THEY TEACH US TO PRAY

A Biographical ABC of the Prayer Life

REGINALD E. O. WHITE

With a Foreword by
F. Townley Lord

HARPER & BROTHERS PUBLISHERS
NEW YORK

To
G.M.W.,
L.E.W.,
G.A.W.

FOREWORD

By F. Townley Lord, D.D., D.Litt.

THE AUTHOR KINDLY ALLOWED ME TO SEE THIS STUDY of prayer in manuscript form. Browsing among the manuscript pages I found myself growing eager to possess the printed volume.

Mr. White's treatment of his theme is unusual. It is based on two convictions; (1) That prayer lies at the root of religious experience and power; (2) That the meaning of prayer is best understood, and its power vitally apprehended, through fellowship with those who pray and by reflection on their example. Hence his method of selecting great figures from the Bible, a biographical survey culminating in two fine chapters on Jesus. He develops his theme in a series of studies with headings following the alphabet: "The Argument of Prayer", "The Benefits of Prayer", "The Condition of Prayer", and so on. Should any reader wonder whether such a deeply spiritual theme lends itself to alphabetic treatment it may be recalled that there is Biblical precedent for it. The twenty-two stanzas of Psalm 119, and the portrait of a good woman in Proverbs 31, for example, both follow a plan suggested by the consonants of the Hebrew language.

The reader may test these chapters by three considerations: What have they to say to preachers and teachers who want to understand and expound the Biblical teaching on Prayer? What have they to say to those (and they are many) on the look-out for helps in the devotional life? What guidance do they offer to those who find difficulties in prayer? In all three respects *They Teach Us to Pray* makes a valuable contribution to devotional literature.

Mr. White's analysis of the characters he brings before us is scholarly and full of insight. On this ground alone—

appreciation of Biblical figures—this book makes excellent reading; but there is much more. He has a way of lifting a problem of the devotional life out of its ancient setting and giving it a present-day meaning. Running through these chapters is the central theme, well expressed, for example, in the study of Moses, that "the difference prayer makes is the difference between our inadequacy, our uncertainty, our discouragements and the divine strength, illumination, joy which are given to him who prays".

This is a book of spiritual enrichment. Its clear and flowing style, its analysis of religious experience in many periods of Bible history, its insight into the problems of the spiritual life focus our attention on communion with God, which is the ultimate meaning of prayer. It is a notable addition to the literature of devotion and it should gain for Mr. White a large and appreciative public.

F.T.L.

1957

CONTENTS

PART I

GREAT MEN OF PRAYER

PART II

THE MASTER OF PRAYER

9

PART I

GREAT MEN OF PRAYER

ABRAHAM: THE ARGUMENT OF PRAYER

"THEY TEACH US TO PRAY": AND YET, OF COURSE, IN THE usual meaning of the word—the imparting of knowledge by one mind to another—prayer cannot be "taught". Like love and faith, like the response of the soul to beauty and the experience of the joy of God, prayer has to be known at first hand or it is not known at all. The truth about it can be reached only from within, and attempts to analyse, expound, discuss the life of prayer from without, as an abstraction—"a feature of the religious life"—are bound to fail because the point of view is wrong. But what cannot, in any academic sense, be "taught" may still be shared. As love and beauty are best known through contact with the loving and beautiful, so prayer is best learned through fellowship with those who pray, and through reflection upon their example. It was "as Jesus was praying in a certain place, when He ceased" that one of the disciples was stirred to ask Him "Lord, teach us to pray" (Luke 11: 1). It follows that any study of prayer, if it is to be adequate, practical and helpful, must be biographical. We learn to pray by listening to those who do.

There is another, and a deeper, reason for "biographical" study of the life of prayer. Prayer lies at the heart of all experience of God: in prayer God is known, and met, and touched.

13

In prayer all our knowledge about God kindles into life; our understanding of the Scriptures gains personal illumination and power; our whole conduct and career passes consciously under the divine judgement. In prayer the soul is moulded and attuned to fresh obedience and confronted with new duties, our relationship to others is seen in new perspective, and conscience grows tender again. In prayer vision is clarified, the horizons are broadened, the goal becomes better defined, and the inner resources by which the soul lives are replenished from eternal springs of power, hopefulness and peace. Prayerless religion is mere theory. Prayer gives to inherited knowledge, custom and faith their present life and meaning. As a philosopher might say, in prayer the whole spiritual life of man finds its moment of truth. A study of prayer is therefore inevitably a study of God, of the soul, and of their innermost relation one to another. Nothing really vital to personal religious life and experience is outside its scope. That is why all cannot be known at once, and from one angle; and why, again, study of the prayer-life should be biographical. We cannot hope to catch the truth of so profound and personal a matter except as we watch and listen to men of prayer to whom God was real, and near, and attentive. And amongst such men, Abraham ranks very high indeed.

I

"*And Abraham drew near and said, Wilt Thou also destroy the right- eous with the wicked? Peradventure there be fifty righteous within the city: wilt Thou also destroy and not spare the place for the fifty righteous that are therein? That be far from Thee to do after this manner, to slay the righteous with the wicked: and that the righteous should be as the wicked, that be far from Thee: Shall not the Judge of all the earth do right? . . . And Abraham answered and said, Behold now I have taken upon me to speak unto the Lord, which am but dust and ashes: Per- adventure there shall lack five of the fifty righteous: wilt Thou destroy all the city for lack of five? . . . And he spake unto Him yet again, and said, Peradventure there shall be forty found there . . . And he said unto Him, Oh let not the Lord be angry and I will speak: Peradventure there shall be thirty found there . . . And he said, Behold now I have taken upon me to speak unto the Lord: Peradventure there shall be twenty found there . . . And he said, Oh let not the Lord be angry, and I will speak yet but this once: Peradventure ten shall be found there . . ."*

GENESIS 18: 23f.

WITH WHAT PERSISTENCE, AND PERSUASIVENESS, ABRAHAM could pray! He reasons with God as one long used to converse with the Most High, as indeed he was. Abraham travelled north, south, east and west, within and beyond the land of promise, always listening for the inward Voice that directed his steps, and marking the stages of his pilgrimage with altars for his milestones. "Abraham journeyed . . . and he built an altar": that might well have been his epitaph, did he not already possess a better—"He was called the friend of God" (James 2: 23). Apart altogether fr... the accident of history that puts him first, no one has more right to head the list of men of prayer of the Old Testament than this man, whose whole life (except for one or two moments of weakness) was one long experience of two-way communion, of listening and worship, speaking and being spoken to, in that inner conversation which is the highest form of prayer.

Yet it is not practice alone which gives to Abraham's prayer its persuasiveness: it is intercession. He is praying for others, above all, for Sodom! The wicked city, about to reap the terrible harvest which its wild ways had sown, would not thank Abraham for his prayers, nor was there much about her people to encourage Abraham to intercede for their deliverance. But he prays, nevertheless, out of a noble compassion, and perhaps with a feeling of helplessness, a sense that this was all that he could do for so stubborn and rebellious a community. And with him, as with so very many who have trod

15

the path of prayer, intercession became the gateway to fullest communion.

Often enough we kneel to pour out our complaint, our need, our confession, our hopes and hunger before the Lord, and rise feeling that something was missing, some warmth, and lifting of the heart, to assure us we were heard. Sometimes prayer as a whole becomes difficult because we are so concerned with ourselves. The remedy is obvious and simple: to learn unselfishness at the mercy seat. To remember and to plead the cause of others is to enter into a new experience of the intimacy and power of prayer. "The Lord turned the captivity of Job when he prayed for his friends: also the Lord gave Job twice as much as he had before" (Job 42: 10).

This is especially so when intercession is winged by personal concern and affection. In Sodom dwelt Lot, the nephew with whom Abraham had journeyed from Haran, and with whom not long before he had divided the land. Deep concern for one to whom he felt bound by kinship, and doubtless also by a sense of responsibility, gave urgency to his plea and skill to his lips: when he pleaded for the city to be spared for ten, Lot and his wife, the two daughters and their families (Genesis 19: 14) were vividly before his mind. No prayers are so eager or so bold as those we offer for our loved ones.

The boldness is wonderfully mingled with humility. At one moment Abraham almost expostulates with "the Judge of all the earth" about what is fitting and right: at the next he cries with a returning sense of his own daring, "Behold, now, I have taken upon me to speak unto the Lord, which am but dust and ashes". We are bidden to come with boldness, but the throne to which we come remains a throne of grace, before which neither asserted claims nor pretended merit can have any fitness. Everything that may be granted, and the invitation to come and make request, are all of mercy, the free and undeserved favour of our God.

The true spirit of our approach is wonderfully expressed in

16

the model prayer. Ignorant, superstitious fear and presumptuous familiarity with God are alike avoided in the simple "Our Father" which brings God to our side, "which art in heaven" which lifts God again to His eternal throne. If from our prayer the former element, the "full assurance of faith", is lacking we shall never find that restful confidence which makes prayer a deep and renewing joy. If the latter element is lacking, the sense of God's holy majesty, we shall never be subdued and exalted with the consciousness of immeasurable privilege and mercy.

II

It is necessary to bear in mind the intercessory character of Abraham's prayer, and its spirit of mingled boldness and humility, for otherwise to speak of his "argument" with God will seem harsh, and inaccurate. Yet argument there was, behind and within and beneath his prayer, and the fact is deeply instructive.

The argument *behind* the prayer is the whole character of the man. It is always so, and this is one of the most searching truths about prayer. It is not the "what" or the "how" that matters most about any prayer, but the "who". Of course no worthiness or labour of ours can move the heart of God to listen more graciously to our petition: we cannot by our piety persuade God to be more lovingly attentive than He already is. But there is more to be said than that. We are able to ask aright, and God is able to give with safety, only when the heart behind the prayer is a heart schooled in God's ways and surrendered to His will.

Two things said of Abraham in this chapter light up this truth for us. One concerns his ready hospitality to the divine Visitors. Something more than customary Eastern politeness to the wayfarer lies behind the elaborate welcome which Abraham afforded his Guests: somehow, and at some time, he perceived that the Lord had visited him again, and as ever the heart and home of the patriarch were wide open to the divine approach. It is a simple parable of a profound truth. We miss the answer to half our prayers simply because when God comes, with the gift we asked, He finds no entrance, no welcome, no expectancy.

The other comment upon Abraham lies in the glowing words of the Lord: "Shall I hide from Abraham that thing which I do? For I know him, that he will command his children and his household after him, and they shall keep the way of the Lord. . . ." *I know him*, what a tribute from the lips of God! Abraham is one whom God can trust with His secrets, upon whom God can rely both for his own obedience and for his influence over others. It would not be safe, sometimes, for God to grant us our requests. We ask for power, but power might make us conceited and unusable; we pray for success, but success might turn our heads. We might, like Saul, ask great things while we are little in our own eyes, but when we receive them forget whence they came and what they are for, so that the answer to our prayers could leave us poorer than we were. A heart ready and reliable is the only ground upon which to build a prayer life that shall be persuasive and prevailing. The character of the one who prays always sets a limit upon the answer God can give.

III

The argument *within* Abraham's prayer was a reasoned appeal based upon the whole character of God. "That be far from Thee, to do after this manner, to slay the righteous with the wicked: and that the righteous should be as the wicked, that be far from Thee: shall not the Judge of all the earth do right?" And when Abraham obtains the assurance that the city will be spared for fifty righteous, he presses home the plea based upon God's faithful justice—"Peradventure there shall lack five of the fifty righteous, wilt thou destroy all the city for lack of five?" Not his own wish, nor his own pity for the doomed community, nor even his own concern for Lot, but the known character of God is the basis of his supplication. Again we are reminded of the model prayer: "Our Father . . . give us . . . bread, forgive us . . . lead us not into temptation . . . deliver us from evil." What else should children ask, but food, forgiveness, shelter, and help out of trouble?—what else are fathers for? The petitions arise naturally from the known character of Him to whom they are addressed.

This is precisely the point of the answer of Jesus to the disciples' request "Lord, teach us to pray". The Master replied, "If a son shall ask bread of any of you that is a father, will he give him a stone? Or if he ask a fish, will he for a fish give him a serpent? Or if he shall ask an egg, will he offer him a scorpion? If ye then, being evil, know how to give good gifts unto your children: how much more shall your heavenly Father give the Holy Spirit [Matthew has: 'give good things'] to them that ask Him?" Here is the argument of faith, in relation to prayer: it deduces from decent fatherhood in frail and sinful men a perfect fatherhood in God who made them; and then deduces from His perfect fatherliness with what confident and expectant faith we may seek our needs from Him.

Sometimes it is God's character as revealed in His consistent ways that is the basis of the reasoning of faith: "If God so clothe the grass of the field . . . shall He not much more clothe you?" Sometimes it is God's character as shown by what He has already done that provides the standing ground of confidence: "He that spared not His own Son, but delivered Him up for us all, how shall he not with Him also freely give us all things?" And often it is the character of God expressed in His promises that forms our prayer and encourages our asking: "And now, O Lord God, thou art that God, and thy words be true, and thou hast promised this goodness unto thy servant: therefore now let it please thee to bless the house of thy servant, that it may continue for ever before thee: for thou O Lord hast spoken it." (2 Samuel 7: 28, 29.) In each case attention is directed away from ourselves and our desires—or deserts—to God and His constancy of love, His steadfastness of character. Faith ever reasons from the God we know to the goodness which we seek. To put the point in a different way: we believe, not as we sometimes rather loosely say, in the efficacy of prayer, but in the graciousness of God. On that all prayer experience rests.

Those familiar with the ancient forms of prayer which are part of the Church's treasury of devotion, will have realised how often the most moving prayers proceed upon just such an argument of petition as Abraham's. The so fitting petitions in the prayer for each day—"defend us . . . with thy mighty power, and grant that this day we fall into no sin, neither run into any kind of danger, but that all our doings shall be ordered by thy governance, to do always that is righteous in thy sight . . ." gain immeasurably in meaning and power when we lift them to God in the words "O Lord our heavenly Father, Almighty and everlasting God, who hast safely brought us to the beginning of this day . . ." The reminder of God's everlastingness, His Fatherly care, and His inexhaustible strength prepare us for the request in faith, but what depth of confidence is added when we recall that it is the same God who has brought us to the beginning of this day, for which now we ask His grace.

The prayer for times of trouble "Defend us thy humble servants in all assaults of our enemies, that we, surely trusting in thy defence, may not fear the power of any adversaries, through the might of Jesus Christ our Lord" is offered with so much more humility and trust when it is addressed to God "Who art the author of peace and lover of concord, in knowledge of whom (not in earthly security) standeth our eternal life, whose service (not the licence and ease of our self-chosen way) is perfect freedom"—at every point the petitions for

20

safety are balanced by recognition that that safety must be as He wills.

Perhaps the best example is another, lesser known prayer—— "O God who art and wast and art to come, before whose face the generations rise and pass away: age after age the living seek thee, and find that of thy faithfulness there is no end. Our fathers in their pilgrimage walked by thy guidance and rested on thy compassion; still to their children be thou the cloud by day, and the fire by night. . . ."

Over-careful choice of words may rob prayer sometimes of its true fervour and spontaneity, but there is more in the form of such petitions than just beauty. There is the application of Abraham's lesson that what matters first in prayer is not our needs and our pleadings but what God has revealed to us of His character, will and purpose. Many of our doubts and disappointments about prayer, many of the world's gibes at our "escapism", would be answered if our prayers were oftener upon this level of breathing back to God in praise and supplication His own revelation of Himself and His own promises of grace. And certainly our prayer experience would grow in power and confidence.

IV

The argument *beneath* the prayer of Abraham is but the extension to the whole field of our devotion of this principle, that what we ask of God should arise from what we know of God's character, and ways. It governs not merely the form of prayer, but in the last resort the very impulse and habit and practice of prayer and all that belongs to it, worship, supplication, confession, intercession, praise. The simple logic of faith underlies it all: God being what He is, it *follows* I should pray. Prayer is nothing more than faith becoming articulate, belief finding utterance. I believe that God cares—it follows that I share my cares with Him; I believe that God is merciful—it follows that I come to Him for pardon; I believe that God reveals Himself to those who seek Him—it follows that I seek His will to guide my steps.

To "believe" in God and not to pray is paradox, contradiction—much worse, it is a dangerous self-delusion. Whatever we may profess, or persuade ourselves is true, we do not believe in God if we never speak to Him, nor seek His grace, nor call upon His mercy. Prayer *is* faith—finding expression. When this is clearly, convincingly seen, all "motives", "exhortations" and "persuasions" to pray are seen to be largely irrelevant. Those who truly believe *do* pray, though perhaps not as often, as wisely, as unselfishly, as effectively, as they might.

This is the argument beneath all worship, thanksgiving, surrender, all prayer for mercy, grace, guidance, or power, and intercession for others. In the widest sense it is *the* argument of prayer: God is gracious, tender, loving, true—*therefore* I do, and I will, seek His face.

v

A word must be added concerning the answer Abraham received, lest any impression be left that prayer is "arguing God into doing something" which He might not otherwise do. There is something even in God's answer that seems in keeping with the reasoning of faith. The city was not spared: to that extent the argument did not succeed. But Lot was delivered, and that after all was the deepest burden on Abraham's heart. *Abraham received, not what he asked, but what he wanted.* God's refusals are ever of this kind, sweetly reasonable, granting often what we did not seek, because we did not understand, but what He knew would meet our situation more perfectly. For even the highest argument of faith must give way to that supreme Wisdom which best knows both what to give and what withhold, and when to withhold in the very act of giving, and give better than expected by the grace of its withholding.

Thus at the outset of our studies, Abraham has led us at once into a truly vital secret about prayer. For want of it many have missed the true joy of the prayer-life, and some have given up praying. We shall get no further in the experience of prayer unless we take full measure of this insight: prayer is neither a magical formula nor a ritual technique for achieving results in the spiritual world; it is essentially a reasonable, personal relationship. In it, man's faith addresses God's mercy, and the outcome is entirely governed by the character of God who hears and the trustworthiness of the man who asks. *What we know of God, and what He knows about us—these lay the foundation, and set the strict limits, of all our experience of the power of prayer.*

MOSES: THE BENEFITS OF PRAYER

"*And it came to pass as Moses entered into the tabernacle, the cloudy pillar descended and stood at the door of the tabernacle, and the Lord talked with Moses . . . And the Lord spake unto Moses face to face, as a man speaketh unto his friend . . . And Moses said unto the Lord . . . Shew me now thy way . . . shew me thy glory . . . And the Lord said: I will make all my goodness pass before thee. And it came to pass, when Moses came down from mount Sinai . . . that Moses wist not that the skin of his face shone while he talked with him . . . And the children of Israel saw the face of Moses, that the skin of Moses' face shone . . ."*

EXODUS 33: 9-23; 34: 29-35

A STRANGE CONTRADICTION MARKS THE STORY OF THE second Old Testament hero of the life of prayer, a paradox at once puzzling and illuminating. The history of the Old Testament is dominated by the towering figure of Moses. He is a giant in several realms at once, and left an enduring mark not only upon the experience of his own people, but upon the history of mankind, and especially upon the story of man's religious pilgrimage.

On the lowest level, simply as a practical man of affairs, Moses stands without peer. The gifts of vision and leadership, of organisation, decision, judgement and patience which were demanded by the immense task of extricating a band of slaves from their bondage, and planning and carrying out their

24

migration from Egypt to Canaan, largely without their co-operation and in face of their continual "murmuring", were no ordinary endowments. Yet Moses accomplished it without any significant measure of human assistance.

As lawgiver and statesman Moses gave to his disunited and inexperienced flock a legal code and a constitution, a sense of justice and of social responsibility, without which they could never have risen to nationhood; and upon the basis of his laws the Jewish nation lived for a thousand years.

But it is, of course, supremely as a religious figure that we reverence Moses, and feel his surpassing greatness. Through his leadership Israel learned unforgettably the majesty and power of her Redeemer, mightier than the gods of Egypt, Ruler of the earth and sea, Guide through the wilderness, Captain in battle, Giver of manna and water in the desert, and in all things and at all times the Covenant-keeping God.

This last point, the Covenant of God with Israel, is one of the greatest religious conceptions of all time. Other nations in the middle East regarded their relationship to their gods as purely natural, holding that they were descended from the god, and that the god was therefore necessarily and in all circumstances bound to remain their defender and their head. Israel alone among the ancient peoples rose to the idea of a voluntary bond, freely entered into, between the people on the one hand and God upon the other, a Covenant of loyalty, in which men responded by obedience to the gracious offer of Jehovah to be their God. The Covenant was never of course a bargain between equals. The terms were established by God alone, and the initiative was God's: it began in grace. God had saved Israel from Egypt, and unfolded to them His purposes of full redemption, renewing the ancient promises made to Abraham, and assuring of His favour and His presence so long as they on their part should keep His Covenant and remember His commandments to do them.

The terms of the divine Covenant were promulgated at

Sinai, and Israel's acceptance of them was sealed in the Covenant sacrifice at the foot of the mountain. In this way the clear moral and social responsibility to do the holy will of Jehovah was established at the heart of Hebrew religion, and ethical obedience declared to be the condition of all blessing. The failure of the first Covenant, and the inauguration of the new, foretold by Jeremiah and established by Our Lord in the "cup of the New Covenant" show how near to the heart of our faith lies the thought of Covenant relationship.

Detailed investigation of the origin of the idea would carry us very far from our present purpose. What is certain is that it was at Sinai, and at the hand of Moses, that Israel as a whole first received and by sacrifice accepted her Covenant with God. Thus for her existence as a people, for the foundations of her law and national life, and for much that was most creative and enduring in her religion, Israel was immeasurably indebted to this mighty man of old, Moses the servant of the Lord.

I

What kind of man was he—the man behind the achievements? Here lies the paradox: so far as his personal qualities can be discerned beneath the mantle of historic greatness, Moses is a surprisingly unimpressive figure. We have learned of Jesus to value meekness, and to recognise its latent strength. But when it was written of Moses "Now the man Moses was very meek, above all the men which were upon the face of the earth" the quality of meekness had not gained its Christian halo. The story which contains this famous comment upon the man excellently illustrates its meaning. Miriam and Aaron "spake against" Moses, and they said "Hath the Lord indeed spoken only by Moses, hath He not spoken also by us?" We are astonished by such behaviour only because we imagine that something about the man himself would mark him off as different from all others, would intimidate rivals and forestall

26

rebellion. The attempt to "gainsay" him—and by such people —shows our mistake.

A little later, Korah and his confederates similarly seek to usurp Moses' authority, feeling no great disparity between themselves and their leader. There was clearly nothing unchallengeable about Moses' personality; his personal presence, like Paul's long afterwards, was in the eyes of his enemies weak and insignificant.

This impression is confirmed when we remember Moses' response to his call. His earlier attempts to succour his Hebrew brethren in their bondage had ended not only in failure but in most humiliating flight and concealment. The sense of this failure weighed heavily upon him when at the Burning Bush the call came to return to Egypt and deliver Israel. Many and persistent are the arguments with which Moses would evade the task, and "the anger of the Lord was kindled against Moses" whose absorption in his own insufficiencies was threatening to become a hindrance to God's purpose.

So it was throughout the story. His recurrent fears, his shrinking from hard duties, his occasional despondencies, and his sense of failure show how ill-matched, to human judgement, were the man and the task. What depth of feeling, of conflicting anger and despair, breathes through the words: "Moses also was displeased. And Moses said unto the Lord, Wherefore hast thou afflicted thy servant? and wherefore have I not found favour in thy sight, that thou layest the burden of all this people upon me? Have I conceived all this people? Have I begotten them, that thou shouldest say unto me, Carry them in thy bosom . . . I am not able to bear all this people alone, because it is too heavy for me. And if thou deal thus with me, kill me, I pray thee, out of hand, if I have found favour in thy sight; and let me not see my wretchedness."

Here for a brief moment we are allowed to see into the heart of this meek and mighty soul. We discover a personal temperament shrinking and self-distrustful; we find an early experience

27

of noble intentions crushingly defeated, misrepresented, and leaving behind a sense of inferiority; we see a heart laden with heavy burdens and faced with a seemingly impossible commission, ready to resign, despair and die under his lonely responsibility amid the bitter ingratitude of his people. Such was the human instrument by means of which such epoch-making triumphs were achieved.

II

There is no more vivid illustration, no more cogent proof, of the benefits of prayer than this contrast between Moses the man and Moses the maker of history. Quite simply and obviously the difference between the two is the measure of the power of prayer; the "invisible asset" by which this shrinking and discourageable soul was matched for his magnificent work was precisely that which came to him through prayer. "The Lord spake unto Moses face to face, as a man speaketh unto his friend".

Again and again a prayer of Moses is explicitly recorded— at the Burning Bush; when in Egypt the people blame him for their increased burdens; when the waters at Marah are found to be bitter, and again when water of any kind is found to be scarce; at Sinai's solemn convocation, and at Sinai's fearful sin in the making of the golden calf. He prays at the Tent of Meeting, and at the consecration of the completed altar; at the punishment of Taberah, and the leprosy of Miriam. He prays when the people complain of the sameness of the food, at the smiting of the rock, at the report of the spies, at the announcement that he himself will not enter Canaan, and at the request for a glimpse of the promised land. In every emergency, at every disappointment, whenever the way is closed and the burden heavy, Moses turns to God.

Even more impressive than the record of particular prayers is the number of occasions, too great to count, on which we read "And the Lord spake unto Moses, saying . . ." For to

Moses prayer meant listening as well as speaking, and he was constantly receiving instructions, referring every new question and situation to that inner Voice which was his Guide. How exactly the New Testament explains the "little one who became a thousand", the meek soul made mighty, with the words: "Moses endured as seeing Him who is invisible". His sufficiency was of God, who made him able. His resources were wholly and always in his prayer-life.

That above all else is what prayer means—drawing upon divine resources of wisdom, courage, power, understanding, grace, patience, peace, or whatever shall be needed of material, moral, mental or spiritual "supplies" for the doing of our duty and the service of our Lord. Great men of prayer in every age have exhibited this same strange spectacle of insignificant personal attainments combined with mighty spiritual achievements. The explanation is ever the same—that by prayer a man's personal resources of every kind are underwritten, multiplied, inexhaustibly renewed. We bring our few loaves and poor fishes in prayer to our Lord and with them He feeds the multitude. The meek are "mighty through God"— by the power of prayer.

III

This is the great lesson of Moses' experience, but included within it are two especially helpful reminders. In the passage beginning at Exodus 33: 12 Moses seeks from God some reassurance and comfort for his task. "Show me Thy way . . . show me Thy glory" is his eager plea. How else could he hope to succeed in leading Israel forward to Canaan, instructing them in the affairs of faith and nationhood, and governing them with justice and wisdom? He asks to be shown not "my way" but "Thy way"—perhaps because his earlier failure convinced him that "my way" would not do. The task demands a wisdom wholly higher than his own, and guidance far beyond his own poor vision.

The answer he receives is "My presence shall go with thee". He asked instruction, but he gets Companionship. A guide is infinitely better than a signpost, or a map, or even a known way. Often in impatience we ask for these, because we want to see the end from the beginning, but while He kindly veils the future God promises to walk beside us "each step of the way".

Even so the way might daunt the spirit, might well be shadowed and steep and stretch discouraging distances. Moses asks "Show me Thy glory" that the way might seem easy, and the shadows be dispelled. Above the murmuring of the people, the faithlessness of men, the mists of the wilderness, the fears of his own heart, Moses would gaze for a moment on the glory of God, and so inspired would step forward bravely with a memory in his soul beside which all disappointment and disaster would seem unimportant. And God made "all His goodness to pass before him", for the glory of God *is* His goodness.

Prayer brings then, beside resources, revelation. When the way forward is confused, when duty is unclear, the questions throb within our minds, and the problems of discipleship in a chaotic world multiply about us, then prayer brings illumination, a sense of direction, and an inner guidance not to be doubted or gainsaid. When personal relationships get entangled, and the work to which we have sincerely set our hands seems too great for our poor wit or wisdom, then in the hour of prayer a new understanding dawns, the next step becomes plain, and things obscure, ambiguous, uncertain, take on the quality of obvious duty and simple sense. Oftentimes we wonder what we were so puzzled about!

It may well be that not a single new idea rises in the mind, that no overwhelming impulse is experienced; no spectacular vision is vouchsafed. A mind emptied before God may well remain empty. We are promised that He will guide us *in judgement*. The reflective spirit, marshalling all the facts of a situation before God in expectant faith, *does* find that "praying about it" has brought a new simplicity, a new sense of proportion, a new realisation of what is essential and what is simply unimportant, a reminder of the goal and a clearer understanding of the steps that lead in its direction. Sometimes the illumination so gained breaks on the mind with all the force of a totally new directive from God: we feel that God has spoken.

And if the way shown seems too hard, if the soul remains reluctant, if the duty now seen so clearly involves risk and opposition—then our "Show me Thy glory" may bring the blazing certainty of the goodness and faithfulness of God which will send us on our way if not yet rejoicing at least ready to endure and not complain.

IV

The second helpful reminder of the benefits of prayer which the story of Moses offers us, has to do not with the illumination of the mind but with the correction of the mood, and occasionally that is almost as important. As Moses returned from the "Tent of Meeting" where he was wont to hold converse with God, bringing to God the supplications of the people and receiving his instructions for the march, "He wist not that his face shone". Israel knew it, and so did Aaron, and they were afraid. Moses alone remained unconscious of the light that transfigured him, the radiance that clung about his figure, as the season of prayer closed and he returned to the day's tasks. Something appeared in his glance, his bearing, a light in his eye, a smile upon his lips, a relaxing of nervous tension perhaps, a lifting of the brows, a regained poise and serenity of spirit—let no one despise the value of such corrections of the spirit's mood. In such renewal of the peace that is not of this world but borrowed for a while that the world's demands may be more adequately met, the reality and nearness of our approach to God is seen. And those who behold it testify with awe and wonder to the value of communion with God for the healing of the human spirit.

Stephen, in the New Testament, reminds us of this higher reach of prayer experience: "All that sat in the council saw his face, as it had been the face of an angel". We know how that radiant countenance haunted the mind of Saul of Tarsus until he too shared Stephen's faith. But One greater than Stephen, or Moses, "took Peter and John and James and went up into a mountain to pray; and as He prayed, the fashion of His countenance was altered" and He was transfigured before them. Prayer could do that, even for Him whose soul was never once plunged into the faithless gloom that so often overshadows ours.

How much more we need to recapture the radiant joy and shining peace that only come to us when God is very near, and to bear back to our own world and to the darkened lives about us some lingering reflection of a radiance and a glory seen upon the mountain-top. No greater, no more desperate need, faces the modern Church than to re-experience the spiritual trans-figuration that came to the first generation of Christians. It is not impossible for the least of us. "We all, reflecting as in a mirror the glory of the Lord, are changed into the same image, from glory to glory, even as by the Lord, the Spirit."

Resources, revelation, radiance: if we have said nothing so far of the more material benefits of prayer it is not because they are to be despised, as though it were unworthy to pray with Jesus for our daily bread. It is rather because, while the material requests are more familiar, and every believer has his testimony to the wonder of God's answers, it is sometimes forgotten that God would do much more for us that we nor-mally ask—or even think. It is this "much more" that the prayer-experience of Moses so convincingly illustrates. *The difference prayer makes is the difference between our inadequacy, our uncertainty, our discouragement and the divine strength, illumination, and joy which are given to him who prays.* The highest miracle of the prayer-life is not that by it we obtain many different things, but that through it we can be made such very different people. But of that miracle, most of us have very much to learn.

JOSHUA: THE CONDITION OF PRAYER

"*So there went up of the people about three thousand men: and they fled before the men of Ai. And Joshua rent his clothes and fell to the earth upon his face before the ark of the Lord until the eventide, he and the elders of Israel, and put dust upon their heads. And Joshua said, Alas, O Lord God . . . what shall I say when Israel turneth their backs before their enemies . . . And the Lord said unto Joshua, Get thee up; wherefore liest thou thus upon thy face? Israel hath sinned . . . therefore the children of Israel could not stand before their enemies . . . Up, sanctify the people, and say, Sanctify yourselves against tomorrow: for thus saith the LORD God of Israel, There is an accursed thing in the midst of thee, O Israel; thou canst not stand before thine enemies, until ye take away the accursed thing from among you . . . So Joshua rose up early in the morning, and brought Israel by their tribes; . . . and Achan was taken . . . And all Israel stoned him with stones . . . And the Lord said unto Joshua, Fear not, neither be thou dismayed: take all the people of war with thee, and arise, go up to Ai: see, I have given into thy hand the king of Ai, and his people and his city and his land: and thou shalt do to Ai and her king as thou didst unto Jericho and her king.*"

JOSHUA 7: 4–8: 2

MOST OF US THINK OF JOSHUA NOT AS ONE OF THE FORE-most men of prayer, but as a man of action. The picture that springs to mind at the mention of his name is not that of the kneeling saint, but that of the alert and well-armed warrior. He is essentially the soldier, the leader of men, a governor with a firm hand and resolute decision.

33

There is about Joshua nothing of the self-mistrust of Moses, and little of the experience of visions and voices that Abraham knew. His qualities are courage, firmness, energy, shrewdness, leadership and strength. His life was marked more by activity than by anxious self-examination: more by military achievement than by mystical aspiration. So at least the familiar portrait suggests: a man of deeds, an "extrovert", a soldier "and no nonsense".

I

The portrait is not wrong, but it is seriously incomplete. To it must be added three features which reveal another and deeper side to his character. "Moses turned again into the camp: but his servant Joshua, the son of Nun, a young man, departed not out of the tabernacle"; and again, "Moses rose up, and his minister Joshua, and Moses went up into the mount of God" (Exodus 33: 11, 24: 13). We may surely presume that Moses knew well the spiritual quality and personal piety of the young man he chose to wait upon him in that most sacred hour, and to have care of the nation's shrine.

Secondly, we recall that Joshua shared with Caleb the difficult task of seeking to persuade the people that though, as the ten other spies had said, the cities of Canaan were walled to the skies and the people of the land like giants, yet Israel could advance to take the land "for the Lord is with us: fear them not". In this argument with the people's unbelief Joshua seems indeed to have taken the first place. He is to be remembered therefore as a young man of courageous faith.

And thirdly, a fascinating story occurs in Joshua 5: 13–15. Faced with the task of capturing Jericho, the armed threshold of Canaan, with his band of untrained, undisciplined and somewhat unreliable men, Joshua walks alone, within sight of the city, musing upon "ways and means". He finds a man armed, with drawn sword in his hand, apparently barring his way, and soldier-like Joshua at once challenges him: "Art thou for us, or for our adversaries?" only to receive the disconcerting answer: "Nay, but as Captain of the host of the Lord am I now come." Who, apart from Joshua himself, dares claim to be "Captain of the Lord's host"—but the Lord Himself? "And Joshua fell on his face to the earth and did worship, and said unto him, What saith my Lord unto his servant? And the Captain of the Lord's host said unto Joshua, Loose thy shoe from off thy foot for the place whereon thou standest is holy. And Joshua did so."

Here is the one "vision" (if it might be so described) granted to Joshua; it is his commissioning as conqueror of Canaan, as second-in-command of God's host. Deliberately the commissioning of Moses, Joshua's hero, is recalled in the words "Take off thy shoes . . ." that Joshua might realise the depth of the promise "As I was with Moses so will I be with thee". But equally deliberately the form of the interview is changed: a burning bush upon the wilderness waste for the lonely shepherd, but an armed warrior angel prepared for battle, for the soldier of God. Thus does God fit His comings to the man and to the moment's need; and fittingly does Joshua respond, bowing before his High Command: "What saith my Lord unto His servant?"—What are my orders?

With these features added to the soldierly portrait we realise how balanced was the character of Joshua. The same fine combination of strenuous and resolute courage with deep faith and consecration, of piety with activity, has marked the lives of many outstanding soldiers, from Cromwell and his men to General Gordon and not a few in our own day. If such a man should teach us anything about prayer, as Joshua certainly does, we might expect that it will be something plain, practical, shrewd, austere and probably rather blunt. And so it is, for Joshua's lesson concerns the inescapable condition of prayer: the condition of obedience.

II

The lesson is enshrined in the strange and violent story of the sin of Achan, the defeat before Ai, and the stealing of the devoted thing at Jericho. To understand what seems a harsh act of rough, indiscriminate justice, we must remember the exact circumstances of the time. These were days long before Jeremiah had taught Israel the spiritual value of the individual. In that age the family, the tribe, the clan were the units of society, and when therefore one man's sin was the sin of Israel, and one man's judgement involved himself, his wife, his children and his household in destruction.

Moreover the significance of the "fall" of Jericho, and the reason why the city and all within it were devoted to God, must be recognised. Israel had to learn, once for all, that she entered Canaan not by her own prowess or for her own good, but by the hand of God and for His own purposes. The older generation had learned the same things at the Red Sea and Sinai. The immature tribes and clans must learn to be a humble, worthy and disciplined people. Hence Israel takes Jericho without striking a single blow of which she can boast, and for the same reason of discipline all the spoil, the first fruits of the land, the reward of conquest, are wholly and utterly God's. No plunder is permitted, no lawless revenge, no mad scramble for spoil or slaves. A disciplined people with a high sense of sacred commission and a higher sense of destiny must not descend to a wild rabble of invading brigands. Such a catastrophe would defeat God's plan for Israel. For that matter it would dispel the feeling of religious awe which had fallen upon the Canaanites when the story of the wilderness journey and the crossing of the Jordan had reached their ears, and so bring God's name into contempt—as Joshua urges.

The law then must be rigorously enforced; to disobey was sacrilege, stealing from God. One deed like Achan's, once it was known, could break the discipline of Israel and bring

36

God's plan to naught. Hence the ignominious defeat at the tiny township of Ai. Success now would only make matters worse: pride, self-assurance and greed would evoke still further rebellion. Sin is perilous, prosperity in sin is tragedy.

At the same time a humiliating defeat at the outset of the campaign for Canaan was itself a serious matter for Israel. Much ancient warfare was an affair of morale, a battle of nerves, in which each side sought to frighten the other by war-cries, dances and rumours. Joshua knew the danger of panic among his own people—"the heart of the people melted"—while a sudden realisation by the Canaanite leaders that the Israelites are merely plunderers, like the Philistines, could provoke a swift, united and resolute resistance that might well put Israel to flight. In this light Achan's sin is seen to have something of the nature of treason, national and spiritual betrayal of the interests of his people, and since the whole people and the whole purpose of God are endangered we cannot be surprised at the swiftness of the judgement or the harshness of the penalty. Even Joshua's heart quails at the possibilities, and he pleads—he almost expostulates—with God.

III

Is there, in the whole of Scripture, an answer to prayer that is more abrupt, more searching or more stern than came to Joshua? The soldier is answered in military fashion: "Get thee up; wherefore liest thou upon thy face? Israel hath sinned . . ." This is not the time to pray, but to act. Prayer without obedience is a waste of time. Supplication can never hide evasion, and prayer is never a substitute for doing what God commands. While Israel's sin remains, unconfessed and un-condemned, it is idle for Joshua to plead with God for victory.

That is Joshua's contribution to the ABC of prayer: the condition of successful, powerful, continued prayer is obedi-ence. The harboured evil, the tolerated sin, rises up before us

37

as we kneel. Heaven seems far off, prayer is hard, and no earnestness of speech, no hours of wrestling with God, no multiplication of words, will avail us anything unless it be to make the sin more plain to us and the conscience more oppressed. "If I regard iniquity in my heart, the Lord will not hear me" is the teaching of the whole of the Old Testament, especially emphasised because Israel, like her neighbours, was ever ready to divorce religion from morality, ritual and prayers from character.

The verse just quoted is by a Psalmist, and another poet, Job, echoes the thought: "What is the hope of the hypocrite . . . will God hear his cry when trouble cometh upon him?" The sages agree with the poets, saying in Proverbs: "He that turneth away his ear from hearing the law, even his prayer shall be abomination", and again "Then shall they call upon me, but I will not answer: they shall seek me early but they shall not find me: for that they hated knowledge and did not choose the fear of the Lord: they would none of my counsel: they despised all my reproof."

And poets and sages are joined most emphatically by prophets. Isaiah declares to a religious but unrighteous people "When ye spread forth your hands I will hide mine eyes from you; yea when ye make many prayers, I will not hear: your hands are full of blood." Micah warns of the hiding of the Lord's face from those who "behave themselves ill in their doings", and Jeremiah is told that though the people shall cry unto God, "I will not hearken unto them" and he is bidden "Pray not for this people—thus have they loved to wander".

Zechariah rehearses the persistent refusals of Israel to hearken unto the law of God concerning care for the fatherless, the widow, the stranger and the poor, "stopping their ears and making their hearts like stone lest they should hear the law". He pronounces the fitting penalty: "Therefore it is come to pass that as he cried, and they would not hear; so they cried, and I would not hear, saith the Lord of hosts." Malachi is so sure that God will not accept the worship or hear the prayers of a false and sinful people that he longs that someone would shut the temple doors and let the altar fires go out. This is the Old Testament's reply to the familiar questions about unanswered prayer: "If I regard iniquity in my heart the Lord will not hear me."

The emphasis of the New Testament is upon the complementary truth that the prayer of the sinner for forgiveness, for deliverance from his sin, is heard at once, and with mercy. But the other fact is not obscured. Curiously, it is the blind man cured by Jesus in Jerusalem who gives it best expression: confessing his inability to argue theology with the learned scribes, he is clear in his mind about this at least, and appeals for general confirmation: "We know that He heareth not sinners."

The Apostle James in his letter both underlines it and explains why it is so: "Ye ask, and ye have not, because ye ask amiss that ye may consume it upon your lusts." One reason, then, is because the sinful heart cannot ask aright; the other is because the sinful heart cannot be trusted with the answer. It is not safe for God to grant what sinning hearts request, and the disobedient soon find it fruitless, and forget, or fear, to ask. In this way prayer becomes the sure index to spiritual health, and the guardian of conscience. Sin tolerated, persisted in, defended, "regarded" with composure and delight, makes prayer of no avail. It causes the habit of prayer to wither and die, and the desire of prayer to be destroyed. The New Testament is as clear as the Old that it is the fervent prayer of a *righteous* man that availeth much. "If ye abide in me, and my words abide in you," said Jesus, "ye shall ask what ye will, and it shall be done unto you."

IV

Prayer is the guardian of conscience. This relation of prayer to obedience is obviously a crucial matter; it explains Faber's haunting aphorism "Prayertime is God's punishment

39

time". Achan's sin was withholding what had once been vowed to God, and the result was total defeat—which is significant. But it is not only actual sin, but the evaded duty, the shirked task, which arises before us in the hour of prayer. In Joshua's case it was not even a duty evaded, but one unrealised, unknown, that was laid now upon his heart with imperative urgency. But whether it be wrong condoned, or right evaded, or unrealised, the duty that awaits attention and obedience is in prayertime laid upon our conscience with a force that cannot be denied if the prayer is to continue.

Sometimes the prayer must wait, until the given command has been fulfilled: "When thou bringest thy gift to the altar, and there rememberest that thy brother hath aught against thee, leave there thy gift before the altar and go thy way; first be reconciled to thy brother, and then come and offer thy gift". Here is a second abrupt answer to a misplaced prayer, to set beside that which came to Joshua—"Get thee up", "Go thy way". How *can* the scoffer pretend that prayer is the sentimentalist's escape from hard duty and high endeavour?

How often the prayer "that God will grant" becomes itself the command "to go and do"! We pray for some soul's salvation, and while we pray become acutely aware that we ourselves have never witnessed to that soul. We pray for reconciliation with some offended brother, and sharply remember while we ask that we have not apologised, nor sought his hand. We pray the Lord of the harvest to send forth more labourers into His harvest fields, and the request lays upon ourselves the uneasy self-accusation, why should we ask only that He send somebody else? Many a man, because he prayed, has found himself at the ends of the earth, and many a scheme of far-reaching importance, many a conflict at sacrificial cost, has been initiated because in the hour of prayer conscience awoke to unrealised obligations and challenging duty. *The condition of prayer is obedience. That is the soldierly Joshua's "order of the day": he who forgets it will either be soon reminded, or he will cease to pray.*

GIDEON: THE DARING OF PRAYER

"*And the hand of Midian prevailed against Israel: and because of the Midianites the children of Israel made them the dens which are in the mountains, and caves, and strongholds . . . And there came an angel of the Lord, and sat under an oak which was in Ophrah . . . and Gideon threshed wheat by the winepress, to hide it from the Midianites. And the angel of the Lord . . . said unto him, The Lord is with thee, thou mighty man of valour. And Gideon said unto him, Oh my Lord, if the Lord be with us, why then is all this befallen us? and where be all his miracles which our fathers told us of, saying, Did not the Lord bring us up from Egypt? but now the Lord hath forsaken us, and delivered us into the hands of the Midianites. And the Lord looked upon him, and said, Go in this thy might, and thou shalt save Israel . . . have not I sent thee? And he said, Oh my Lord, wherewith shall I save Israel . . . And the Lord said unto him, Surely I will be with thee . . . And Gideon said Alas, O Lord God! for I have seen an angel of the Lord face to face. And the Lord said, Peace be unto thee . . . And the Lord said . . . Throw down the altar of Baal that thy father hath, and cut down the grove that is by it . . . And Gideon . . . did as the Lord had said. And the Lord said unto Gideon, The people that are with thee are too many . . . Proclaim in the ears of the people saying, Whosoever is fearful and afraid let him return . . . By the three hundred men that lapped will I save you . . . And the three companies blew the trumpets and brake the pitchers, and held the lamps in their left hands . . . and they cried, The sword of the Lord and of Gideon . . . and the host fled.*"

JUDGES 6: 2, 11–16, 22–24; 25–40; 7: 1–22

41

THE OUTSTANDING FEATURE OF THE STORY OF GIDEON is the hero's astonishing daring. There is a quality of boldness about his decisions and actions that seems to carry the day by sheer audacity and win through by a kind of consecrated rashness. His motto is everything venture, everything have!

There is for example the incident of the altar and the "grove" of Baal. Israel had gravely backslidden. Jehovah was a "new" God in Canaan, and a God of the mountain and the wilderness; it seemed wise policy to keep on good terms with the gods of Canaan, upon whose goodwill the inhabitants had for centuries depended for the fertility of their soil, their flocks and herds. The "grove" was in reality a sacred post or pole connected with fertility-rites, and the existence at Gideon's home of altar and pole dedicated to Baal is evidence that Gideon's family had acquiesced not only in the widespread disloyalty to Jehovah but in the immoralities of Canaanite religion as well. Gideon's sudden stroke, pulling down the altar and destroying the sacred pole, was a perilous gesture: "because he was too afraid of his family and the men of the town to do it by day, he did it by night" (6: 27)—not for concealment, for the deed is swiftly acknowledged as Gideon's, but that it might not be known until too late. Gideon dares his father's anger and his family's displeasure, the hostility of his townsfolk, and the wrath of the god—and public opinion combined with deep-rooted superstition comprise a dangerous opposition.

It is the audacious, dramatic surprise that wins success. Earlier, an unknown prophet had tried to expostulate, persuade and warn, but had been ignored. Gideon acts, decisively and without warning, and where a campaign to change prevailing opinion might have produced nothing, his *fait accompli* startles the district, stings awake the conscience of his father, settles the issue "overnight", and raises the signal for reform and revival throughout Israel. He risks everything—and wins all.

That is equally true of the incident concerning the army. God had said "The people that are with thee are too many . . . lest Israel vaunt themselves", and in obedience Gideon sends scuttling home "whosoever is fearful and afraid". Twenty-two thousand preferred their safety to their reputation. A second test, of vigilance and preparedness for battle, brings the army down to three hundred, for these alone have the presence of mind to remain upon their feet with their weapons in their hands while they drink of a brook in the enemy's vicinity.

To us, after the event, it seems excellent policy, and knowing that God had so commanded we are confident of the outcome. But to men who saw their numbers dwindling in the face of an enemy "like a plague of locusts for multitude", it must have seemed an insane procedure. The danger of wholesale desertion, once the rot started, was very real, and the peril of disaster that would be blamed only upon Gideon's generalship, was equally so. So very much depended, as we have seen, on numbers, noise, war-cries and dances that could panic an opposing army: even today we do not deal thus leniently with cowards in the front line.

Gideon's obedience here demanded a very special quality of courage, courage that had faith and high responsibility and great daring in it—the rare courage that sets the standards sky-high and sends home those who will not try. It is the audacity of the towering ideal, that refuses to be told "it will never work", "you will lose money", "people will stay away", and all the rest of the temporising excuses by which we weaken our witness to the vision we have seen. It is the daring of a great faith that will keep the flag at the *top* of the mast though only three hundred follow, and prefers to fail in attempting the best than to succeed by compromise and betrayal of the highest. Again the risk was enormous, but the gain was great.

The incident of the spying out of the enemy camp, with Phurah his servant, but without bodyguard or sortie to ensure his safety, reveals the same daring combined with great personal bravery. It is no part of the general's task to penetrate alone beyond the enemy lines to gather information about the enemy's morale. It is, indeed, the superior officer's duty to see that someone more easily spared should run the immense risk of capture and death which spying entails. The knowledge gained was admittedly invaluable. The overheard conversation about the Hebrew barley loaf that overthrew the Midianite tent, and the revealing interpretation which betrayed a loss of confidence that portended—and caused—crushing defeat, were worth battalions to Israel. Even so the consequences of discovery would have been disastrous, and only the valour and daring of Gideon made the risk worth while.

And the same quality is shown once more, in even more perilous degree, in the incident of the trumpets and the torches. It was brilliant strategy, the use of the psychological approach to spread alarm and confusion—a gigantic bluff, in fact—to "surround" the enemy camp with men bearing torches hidden in pitchers, and trumpets to their lips, and at a given signal to smash the pitchers, toss the torches, blare the trumpets in one reeling crescendo of menace and destruction. No wonder the Midianite camp was thrown into chaos, and the vast army fled in suicidal confusion. From that stroke of genius flowed victory, a general rising of Israel against the invader, and peace for forty years.

But here again the undoubted success serves to hide the fearful risk that was taken. To string out his handful of men around the multitude of Midianites, setting his forces in the most vulnerable array imaginable, and leaving himself without reserves or retreat, would seem to any commander the height of folly. One whisper of the truth in a Midianite ear would have meant the end not only of Gideon and the three hundred, but of Israel's independence. Here, for the fourth time, everything depends on the audacity of the move: and by sheer daring, and nothing else, it brilliantly succeeds.

II

When, with this description of Gideon freshly in mind, we turn back to the opening scene of his story, it is difficult to recognise the same man. When first the angel of the Lord comes upon him, Gideon is a somewhat sorry figure, and his mood epitomises that of the whole people. Israel have built themselves holes and caves in the mountains, hide-outs and strongholds for refuge from the raids of Midian. Year after year crops and cattle have been lost, homes destroyed, and the people flee on the approach of danger. Gideon threshes wheat by the winepress to hide it from the Midianites: all is concealment, timidity, inactivity, and complaint.

The angel's salutation "The Lord is with thee, thou mighty man of valour" provokes the impatient outburst "Oh my Lord, if the Lord be with us, why then is all this befallen us? and where be all his miracles which our father told us of, saying, Did not the Lord bring us up from Egypt? but now the Lord hath forsaken us, and delivered us into the hands of the Midianites." We notice his doubt—"If!" his challenge—"Where?" his question—"Why?" his sullen conclusion, dogmatically asserted, "The Lord hath forsaken us". Gideon is the typical youth of every generation, ready to argue even with angels, openly casting doubts upon the faith of his fathers because the old ideas "no longer work". He demands a religion that is relevant to new needs, a God who does things now, and not only yesterday. But—still the typical young man—he *does* nothing, except question, challenge, criticise, complain, and despair. That was the mood of Israel: and perhaps the word of the angel was intended, if angels *can* be playfully ironic, to make Gideon see himself, hiding behind the winepress—"a mighty man of valour!"

At any rate the answer of the angel to Gideon's challenge is the answer of God to every generation's querulous complainings: "Go, in this thy might . . . *Thou* shalt save Israel".

45

Faced with that challenge to stop whining about what God should do, or what others should attempt, and to go himself and do, Gideon is suddenly shy and reluctant: "How can I save Israel . . . I am the least in my father's house"—what about my brothers! We admire his outspokenness, we admire his humility, we sympathise deeply with his impatience with mere talk about a God of the past: but we cannot help seeing his weaknesses. He will complain without attempting, blame others but not himself, despair without trying, demand that God does something without realising that God's tools are men.

What can any young man, keeping his feet warm upon his father's hearth, hiding his self-pitying head behind the wine-press—what can such a young man know of the revelation that came to Abraham venturing out into unknown lands at God's bidding? What can such a young man hope to learn of the experience that came to Moses, confronting Pharoah in God's name and carrying God's flock across the wilderness? or of the strength that came to Joshua, fighting the Lord's battles and conquering the Lord's land? What use can there be in sitting at home with folded hands and bowed head, and *wishing* that the excitements and experiences of the pioneers would come to one's own hearth? The first answer to "Where is the God of our fathers?" is, "Where is the faith, and venturing, of our fathers?"

Gideon found his answer, and all his answers, in the angel's clear command: "Go, in this thy might." This is not irony, it is the prophetic present tense, to which what God has said shall surely be, already is. And immediately Gideon's bewailing gave place to boldness, his despair to daring. The situation which, lacking a personal response to God, seemed hopeless and unchangeable, now becomes a challenge to energetic determination and resolute action. The transforming factor is the re-introduction of God, the living, active, commissioning God, in direct touch with an obedient soul. When God and His man make contact, history is at a turning-point.

46

III

Yet the intervention of God in Gideon's experience apparently involved even less of withdrawn and sustained prayerfulness than it did in Joshua's case, and some might think it strange to include Gideon at all among the men of prayer, so little is said directly of any supplication or communion. But the times, the attitudes, the recorded words, are not the essence of the prayer-life, and in several ways we are made to understand that Gideon did certainly know that inner relation to God which is the prayer of the heart and the heart of prayer.

As much as any man in Scripture Gideon felt upon his soul the command to go and do, and with it the sublime assurance of "might" conferred to enable him to achieve. In that sense of commission and enduement he lived and ventured; he knew the hand of God was upon him, and that does not come to prayerless men.

Dimly, it is true, as the immaturity of the times necessitated, but none the less truly, Gideon faced out with God the problem of his own unworthiness. The gift he would offer, in simple hospitality, becomes before his eyes at the touch of the angel's staff a smoking sacrifice of a kid of the flock, and reading its meaning Gideon cries "Alas, O Lord God! for because I have seen an angel of the Lord face to face." Swiftly comes the re-assurance: "Peace be unto thee; fear not: thou shalt not die." And in memory of the moment when his sacrifice was accepted and his confession was met with peace, Gideon built an altar and called it "The Lord is Peace". Here again is the timeless note of a man who knows the Lord.

Gideon's boldness in action did not save him from moments of inward misgiving and fear. It is significant of the depth of his inner life that he carries his doubts straight back to God who called him, and shares his misgivings not with his friends and colleagues, but with the Lord. The story of the fleece has touched the hearts of God's servants in every age, for few have attempted anything for God who cannot tell of their own "fleeces" and prayers for some confirming sign. By the double sign of the dew upon the fleece alone, and of the dew upon the floor around it, God grants to Gideon the renewed sense of His continued command and His unchanging favour. Both Gideon's seeking and God's answering assure us that the man we are studying knew the deep things of God. At each step, too, Gideon's ear is open to the divine bidding; the attack upon Baal's altar, the whittling down of the army, and the spying episode are all undertaken in simple and direct obedience to God's word. If the first lesson in prayer is to speak simply with God, the second is surely to let God reply. Gideon knew how to wait and hear what God the Lord would say.

It would be fanciful, with so brief a story before us, to attempt to trace the development of Gideon's spiritual life. But we can at least measure the distance Gideon has travelled with God when we compare the first argumentative reaction to the angel's words, with the sudden glimpse of him given us outside a Midianite tent, as he hears the promise of victory in the conversation of the soldiers: "And it was so, when Gideon heard the telling of the dream, and the interpretation thereof, *that he worshipped* . . ." That bowed head and thankful heart acknowledging God's promise tell us more about Gideon's spirit than long recorded prayers might have done. The incidental way in which the reference is made helps us to feel again the simplicity and sincerity of Gideon's fellowship with God. When we place alongside this the somewhat surprising testimony borne to him by the Midianite soldiers themselves, that into his hand God hath delivered Midian and all the host, we see that even beyond Israel Gideon was known as a man of God, a champion not simply of Israel but of the Lord.

Here then is ample reason for including Gideon among the Old Testament's roll of the men of prayer, despite the brevity of his recorded supplications. And for letting him teach us that one power of prayer is to confer upon the timid spirit an astonishing boldness, and make the despondent daring.

IV

But is that lesson particularly important? No less than twenty-eight references in the New Testament to the boldness of spirit required of, and exhibited by, the Church of the Apostles, suggest that this quality of the man of God may indeed have much more significance than we usually assign to it. It was "when they saw the boldness of Peter and John" that the Jerusalem authorities first awoke to the fact that the crucifixion of Jesus had not ended their troubles. It was the boldness of Paul's preaching that commended him as a true convert first to the Christians at Damascus and again later at Jerusalem. It is recorded that Paul and Barnabas preached boldly at Antioch in Pisidia, and either in Acts or in the Epistles we are told that Paul was equally bold at Thessalonica, at Iconium, at Corinth and before Agrippa. Paul tells us that evidence of the good effects of his imprisonment was to be seen in the new boldness of the Roman Christians in proclaiming Jesus. The same quality in young and eloquent Apollos first attracted the notice of the two who became his teachers, Aquila and Priscilla.

Surely there is counsel here for all who are concerned for the cause of evangelism. What first arrested attention and compelled the world to listen to the first generation of Christians was not so much the content of the message, or the methods of its propagation, or the gifts of the messengers, but their fearlessness, their daring, their refusal to be intimidated, their aggressive spirit of attack, and the audacity of their claims for Christ.

Paul reminds the Corinthians and the Philippians of this characteristic of his ministry, that they might emulate it, and he urges Timothy's deacons to seek the same quality in their

49

work. One reference suggests that boldness was a mark expected to distinguish true leaders of the Apostolic Church, for Paul declares in his own defence, "If others are bold, so am I".

Certainly this is one of the things which the early Church prayed for, and one of the Gifts which the Spirit conferred. At the first outbreak of persecution the Church turned unitedly to prayer, and after rehearsing the facts before the Lord, pleaded "And now, Lord, behold their threatenings: and grant unto thy servants, that with all boldness they may speak the word . . . And when they had prayed, the place was shaken where they were assembled together; and they were all filled with the Holy Ghost, and they spake the word of God with boldness." Others might think Paul bold above most in his witness for the Master, but knowing the inward fears and quakings of his own heart he is not ashamed to urge the Ephesian Church to make it a matter of special prayer that "Utterance may be given unto me, that I may open my mouth boldly . . . that therein I may speak boldly, as I ought to speak".

Finally, the New Testament has much to say of the boldness towards God which lies beneath this fearless front towards the world. "In Christ we have boldness, and access with confidence—We may boldly say, The Lord is my Helper—We may have boldness in the day of judgement—Let us come boldly to the throne of grace—Having boldness to enter into the holiest by the blood of Jesus—cast not away your boldness". It is significant that the scripture thus joins together the daring of great service with the confidence of great prayer: for this is precisely the lesson we learn of Gideon.

True prayer is not the refuge of a cringing spirit, but the armoury of mighty men of valour. That is Gideon's lesson. Only prayer will release us from that fear of men which keeps us silent and consenting in an unbelieving age; from that fear of self which is really a fear of disgracing ourselves by failure; from that unworthy and ignorant fear of God which dreads without trusting, and holds us back from venturing out on His loving promises. Oh that God would drive us all out from behind our winepresses of self-pitying doubts and querulous questionings, "loose in His cause each stammering tongue, and make us faithful, true and *bold*."

JABEZ: THE ESCAPE OF PRAYER

*"And Jabez was more honourable than his brethren: and his mother
called his name Jabez, saying, Because I bare him with sorrow. And
Jabez called on the God of Israel, saying, Oh that thou wouldest bless me
indeed, and enlarge my coast, and that thine hand might be with me, and
that thou wouldest keep me from evil, that it be not to my sorrow! And
God granted him that which he requested."*

1 CHRONICLES 4: 9, 10

JABEZ MIGHT WELL BE DESCRIBED AS A MAN OF PRAYER
alone. His story and his personality are very obscure;
his name appears to be recorded only because of the
memorable prayer with which it is associated. This is a
considerable distinction, even among Bible characters, for
it is usually some added quality or achievement or far-reaching
result which lends significance to their petitions. Jabez is a
man of prayer or nothing!

I

Yet more information is given to us about his story than
at first appears, and it well repays investigation. We know for
example that from his birth his family was overshadowed by
some heavy sorrow—that Jabez was born to trouble, and
reared in unhappiness. No mother would burden her new-
born babe with so forbidding a name unless in bitterness of

soul she has lost all joy of motherhood and can see no hope
of happier days for the child, who thus must bear through all
his life the symbol of her grief. His ominous name and
inauspicious beginning set the key to his story and the mood
of his prayer—"that it be not to my sorrow!"

Of the circumstances of this grief little is told, but we can
discern at least a hint of poverty. Throughout these chapters
of 1 Chronicles we frequently come upon personal names such
as Ephratah, Hebron, Geshur, Penuel, which are more familiar
to us as the names of places. It was natural that under a system
by which every family possessed its own plot of land, and
lived on its own homestead on the ancestral estate, the tiny
hamlets should bear the names of their hereditary owners.
Often in these chapters a person's home village is mentioned
to afford some indication of the wealth, size or influence of the
family concerned. But nothing of this kind is said about
Jabez. He comes into the chapter unheralded and unrelated,
his family belong nowhere, possess nothing. Contrary to law
and custom his family have retained neither lot, portion nor
estate in the land of promise.

This reading of the matter is confirmed by Jabez' prayer:
"Oh that thou wouldest . . . enlarge my coast"—my border,
my possessions. But what can have happened? Was the land
lost through ill-fortune, illness, exploitation, or just neglect?
or was it flung away by vicious conduct, mortgaged for ill-
advised debts, gambled into bankruptcy? In any case poverty
meant in Israel not only insecurity but shame and social
disrespect: that was part of the family sorrow.

But more is plain. Jabez' family name is not given at all.
No reference to his father occurs in the records of Israel,
though there is a family circle. This is a lad officially without
pedigree, without ancestry among the chosen people. When
it is recalled that these records of the Chronicler are almost
certainly those of the Temple registers, and when the importance of family pedigree to Hebrew thought is weighed, it

seems more than probable that the omission is a silence of discretion, the result of some family disgrace, a form of punishment through a social and official ban.

If this is so, and we have here an Israelite name erased as unworthy of a place in Israel's record of its families, then the mother's sorrow is easy to understand, and the name she gave to this new son born to a household in disgrace is amply explained. This interpretation again is strongly confirmed, this time by the ominous implication of the words "Jabez was more honourable than his brethren". Their names are not given, only a side-glance at their dishonour, in the context of which Jabez' character, and especially his prayer, is made by the Chronicler to shine the brighter. Jabez is remembered as an exception in that evil family, the exception even in his own generation of it.

Thus then we piece the story together. The evil ways which had ruined the family fortunes, broken the mother's heart, brought shame and disgrace upon the fathers, had descended also to the sons, and continued to blight the life and honour of the home—except for one lad who stands up against the drift, rebels against the evil entail, and cries to God for deliverance from an environment of wickedness and a tradition of sin.

II

Not many can grasp, without a deliberate effort of imagination, the full poignancy of a situation like this. Few know it from first hand, but evangelists, pastors, rescue workers and others who care for souls meet it secondhand in many lives and it presents one of their sorest problems, and one of their most distressing heartaches. The trail of misery and persistent temptation which follows for the children and grandchildren of those who figure in serious criminal cases is rarely realised. And the sense of social inferiority and local persecution which hinders the moral development of young people connected even remotely with ordinary petty offences is often greater than we imagine.

The long shadows cast by a drunken, shiftless, gambling home across the hearts and consciences of the growing children may still darken the later years when circumstances have changed, but people and ideals and judgement of issues are still seen in the half-light of the public-house and the gambling den. The broken home, the atmosphere of selfish social snobbery built upon ruthless materialism, the cynical competition for the world's prizes that crowds out all altruism and gentleness—these warp the young soul less obviously but no less powerfully, and make the cry to God for help no less desperate—if ever it is raised.

These are the extreme cases. Of the same kind, though in less degree, is the indifference, condescension, or sometimes active hostility which a young Christian may face within his own home, even when that home is from every other point of view a good home. The new convert, full of his new-found faith and joy, and eager to testify, runs against the current of his family and his circle, and though the experience may make for strong character and great independence of spiritual judgement, it is at a high price of loneliness, doubt, friction and sometimes very real persecution where it hurts most.

"A man's foes shall be they of his own household": it need not be so, it should not be so, in the light of after experience it may be seen to have contributed much to strengthen character. But to many an eager young Christian heart it seems that the hostility of the home goes back for several generations, leaving an entail of specially strong temptation, impaired health, family traditions, inherited situations, and poor repute which together make up a fierce test of Christian faith and spiritual victory.

All this must be pictured in the case of Jabez, as the dawn of manhood brings its bitter realisation of things dimly guessed in boyhood. He grew to understand the family's poverty, with its handicap to the young life. He became aware of the social disgrace of a bad tradition, only too faithfully followed by his brethren who thus justify and strengthen the evil repute that taints them all. He carried the memory of a father who is no boyhood's hero and youth's companion but someone regretted, blamed, apologised for. He shared the sense of a sorrow that clouded all his childhood and bowed in grief the head of his mother who had probably borne more of the shame than did those who were responsible.

Behind all this, warning, frightening, inescapable, lay the knowledge that in his own physical and emotional make-up, in his temperament and cast of mind, in his inborn tastes and trends of character there were those elements which came down to him from an evil past, colouring all his outlook and shaping his inmost thoughts. Such would not indeed determine his life beforehand, as some would have us believe. But certainly they set for him his own special problems of conduct and character, constituting the strength of his temptations, laying down for him the direction in which his fiercest battles will be fought, and altogether designing the difficult stage upon which he must wrestle for a character of his own. For it is beyond dispute that heredity and environment do thus provide the context in which our present lives are set, do determine what shall be our peculiar problems, and provide both the weaknesses which we must learn to overcome, and the weapons which we must learn to handle.

Jabez' prayer has this deep and immensely important significance. It is the prayer of a man who realises his soul's urgent peril from a past of shame and an environment of temptation, from a situation and a social context he did not create, from a set of circumstances inimical to his highest welfare yet beyond his power to change. And it contains the Bible's answer to the so-called tyranny of heredity and environment: bringing to bear upon the two greatest forces that can destroy life at its first spiritual budding, the almighty power of God released through prayer.

III

Jabez' spiritual loneliness lends urgency to his request: "Bless me, even me." "Lord, amidst this sorry tale of sin and godlessness single me out, Lord remember me." It is a pathetic plea, but full of courage, especially in the long centuries before Israel had learned God's care for the individual. But Jabez knows where help is to be found. "I am poor and needy, yet the Lord thinketh upon me: Thou art my help and my deliverer, make no tarrying, O my God" is the echo of Jabez' prayer in a Psalm he might well have written.

Yet Jabez is not selfish in his supplication, though he is thus intensely personal. He desires to restore the family name and fortunes in Israel, to possess again the ancestral home and land, and to give to his clan a place in the sacred destiny of God's people. "Oh that thou wouldest enlarge my border" implies all this, and in view of the story can we blame Jabez for materialism and worldly ambition? He would repair the ruin of the past, materially and morally, and renew the hopes of health and happiness for future generations—that none of his sons might be called "Sorrowful" in their turn.

Most urgent and revealing of all comes the prayer, "Oh that thine hand might be with me, and that thou wouldest keep me from *the* evil, that it be not to my sorrow". All his fear of slipping back to the old ways, of ending as the rest had ended, is in that cry. So also is the sense of personal weakness, of instability, of the need for a stronger hand to hold him. And behind it is the open-eyed realisation that the root cause of the long experience of trouble and ruin lay not in misfortune or injustice but in the moral and spiritual decay of the family, from which he himself, apart from God's help, could not hope to be immune. Jabez' prayer is brief, but it is born of long, long thought.

An example like this of Jabez sets in new light the prayer which Jesus taught us: "Lead us not into temptation, but

57

deliver us from evil". It is the deliberate deployment of divine aid in a situation that, humanly speaking, is hopeless and irredeemable. When past history and present surroundings alike besiege the citadel of the soul, what help is possible but from above?

"There hath no temptation taken you but such as is common to man: but God is faithful, who will not suffer you to be tempted above that ye are able; but will with the temptation also make a way to escape, that ye may be able to bear it" (1 Corinthians 10: 13). There lies the great lesson Jabez teaches in this ABC of prayer-experience. The avenue of prayer is the divine way of escape from every imprisoning pressure of temptation, heredity, environment, inborn weakness, and the consequences of one's own or others' sins.

Yet it is vital to add that the *Escape* is not always by *Flight*. Sometimes God delivers *out* of a situation fraught with spiritual peril, sometimes He delivers *in* it. The saints in Caesar's household, the disciples among Herod's servants, and every lonely struggling Christian set in circumstances or amid family, workmates or associates hostile to his soul, have learned the secret of finding escape *within* a difficult situation, not by running away from it. Occasionally it is right to run away, to "Flee youthful lusts", to "make no provision for the flesh"; but the stronger, and more useful witness may be to stay put and keep clean. Jesus prayed: "I ask not that Thou shouldest take them out of the world, but that Thou shouldest keep them from the evil".

The escape route of prayer, in other words, is not a form of cowardice or evasion. It is the retreat to another environment, within which the soul finds shelter without losing contact with the outside world, or shelving its responsibilities. The writer of the 91st Psalm speaks as though he expected that God would in all circumstances keep him immune from trouble, and secure from all outward attack and distress: "There shall no evil befall thee . . . it shall not come nigh thee". But at the close of the Psalm, in which God answers the confidence of the Psalmist, a deeper note is struck—"I will be with him *in* trouble". And this is, in fact, the suggestion of the poet's opening statement: "He that dwelleth in the secret place of the Most High shall abide under the shadow of the Almighty. I will say of the Lord, He is my Refuge . . ." Here again is the inner environment, the secret place, into which the soul withdraws and finds deliverance while yet in contact with that outer world where pestilence, arrows and destruction threaten.

The New Testament counterpart of this Old Testament truth of the power of the soul to live in its own spiritual world by the "retreat" of prayer, is admirably expressed in a phrase which Paul uses hundreds of times but nowhere more aptly than in the address of his letter to the Colossians. Colosse was in Phrygia, and "the Phrygians are a nation born and intended to be slaves" according to ancient testimony, stigmatising a craven, untrustworthy, shifty spirit. Yet Paul writes to the little Christian community there as those who are "*in* Christ *at* Colosse". Rome, Corinth, Ephesus, Colosse—all were difficult places in which to maintain faith and purity of soul. But the Christian was "in Christ" as well as in the pagan world: and the inner, secret environment in which the soul breathed a purer, diviner air, was the Gospel's "way of escape" by which the believer found deliverance. Abiding in Christ, the soul is safe, and towards that saving truth Jabez was already looking when he sought in God a refuge from the evil that encompassed him.

IV

"And God granted him that which he requested." The existence of the record is its own evidence that Jabez redeemed the family's fortunes and established his own name in Israel. But one striking detail is added in Chapter 2: "The families of the scribes . . . dwelt at Jabez". It is impossible to disentangle the dating of the various genealogies in these chapters, but it seems sufficiently clear that whereas his father's name and homestead had perished from memory, the name of Jabez became attached to a new hamlet in Israel. After his time the "city" of Jabez stood associated in popular memory with Jabez' story and his prayer. And it became the city of the Scribes, the teachers, students, the defenders of the sacred law and the representatives of the Holy Word upon whom must fall the task of educating Israel's young. Is it fanciful to see here some connection with Jabez' early struggles? Did his city become famous as a place of religious training because Jabez had learned through bitter experience the fearful dangers of untaught, mis-spent youth? We cannot say, of course, but the thought is attractive.

Nevertheless, the main fact is incontrovertible. Jabez rose out of his unfortunate background, defying his family's tradition, conquering his environment, victorious over inbred temptations, confounding popular cynicism ("Can any good thing come out of *that* family!"). He achieved this, not by superior advantages, nor by strength of will, nor by the aid of human friends—though the grief of his mother surely counted for something—but through the deliverance wrought by prayer.

Prayer is the key that unlocks every prison of the soul. Because he discovered that, in the specially difficult, seemingly desperate, instance of the prison built by evil environment and tainted heredity, Jabez well deserves a place among the great men of prayer. He is among that countless host of the redeemed who sing with the Psalmist "I waited patiently for the Lord; and he inclined unto me, and heard my cry. He brought me up also out of an horrible pit, out of the miry clay, and set my feet upon a rock, and established my goings. And he hath put a new song in my mouth, even praise unto our God. . . ." *Are we?*

SAMUEL: THE FIDELITY OF PRAYER

"*And all the people said unto Samuel, Pray for thy servants unto the Lord thy God, that we die not: for we have added unto all our sins this evil, to ask us a king. And Samuel said unto the people, Fear not: ye have indeed done all this evil: yet turn not aside from following the Lord, but serve the Lord with all your heart; and turn ye not aside: for then should ye go after vain things which cannot profit nor deliver, for they are vain. For the Lord will not forsake his people for his great name's sake: because it hath pleased the Lord to make you a people unto himself. Moreover as for me, God forbid that I should sin against the Lord in ceasing to pray for you: but I will instruct you in the good and the right way . . . Then came the word of the Lord unto Samuel, saying, It repenteth me that I have set up Saul to be king: for he is turned back from following me, and hath not performed my commandments. And Samuel was wroth; and he cried unto the Lord all night . . . And Samuel came no more to see Saul unto the day of his death; for Samuel mourned for Saul . . . And the Lord said unto Samuel, How long wilt thou mourn for Saul, seeing I have rejected him . . . ?*"

I SAMUEL 12: 19–23; 15: 10, 11, 35–16: 1

SAMUEL WAS THE SON OF A PRAYING MOTHER, AND THE child of answered prayer. His very name is a form of pun upon a Hebrew phrase which means "one asked of God". Again and again in the story of his life we are reminded of the atmosphere of prayer into which he was born. Samuel stands before Israel in several capacities, as Judge, Kingmaker,

61

Prophet and Priest, but in none more consistently than as a man who prayed, persistently and earnestly, for his people.

But Samuel is also the Bible's outstanding example of the meaning of loyalty. Simple fidelity is the foremost quality of his character, and the main source of his influence over Israel's affairs. In the conjunction of these two things, prayerfulness and fidelity, within the compass of one strong character, lies the unique contribution which Samuel can make to the present lesson-course on the secrets of prayer.

I

Of Samuel's loyalty it is hardly possible to speak too highly. It is not too much to say that at the significant moment when Israel first achieved nationhood, and in so doing narrowly missed disaster, she owed everything to her priest-prophet. And especially to his willingness to stand at his post when lesser men would have thrown up the task in righteous indignation—or despair.

Samuel links the period of the Judges, when what government there was in Israel rested on the local and limited leadership of individuals famed for strength, valour or piety, with the period of the kings, when government was supposed to rest upon the national, hereditary and continuous leadership of an anointed Royal House. The demand for a king was new in Israel. It resulted partly from the unfitness of Samuel's sons to inherit their father's work, and partly from a desire to be "like the nations round about"—which probably refers especially to the military and political strength of peoples whose tribal disunity had given place to a national status focussed in the throne.

Samuel seems at first to have regarded the demand as an affront to God, Israel's true King; and to himself as God's representative. He protests vigorously against the departure from old ways. He warns at length of the great dangers involved in granting royal power and prerogatives to any family in Israel. He describes in detail the exactions of labour and taxes that the king will impose. Yet in the end he counsels the new king, anoints him in God's name, and crowns him amid the people's rejoicing.

Nor is this inconsistency: Samuel's own view of the matter remains unaltered. But he knows that a king restrained by a prophet is better than a king without restraint. With remarkable foresight and political maturity he "told the people the manner of the kingdom, and wrote it in a book, and laid it up before the Lord". In this way Saul's kingship came as near as can be imagined (in intention) to the modern conception of a constitutional and limited monarchy, in which the law is above the will of the sovereign. Thus, though he is opposed to the people's decision, Samuel will yet strive to avoid that decision's worst consequences. He will make the best use of a situation he would prefer to avoid. The policy is wrong, his own counsel is discarded, his own position before Israel is compromised, but he will not desert his task, will not give way to self-pity, nor blaze with angry denunciations. Fidelity to God and to his people holds him to his thankless work, though with sad foreboding.

The complete failure of Israel's first king fully justified Samuel's fears. It also provoked in Israel a new crisis, one that might have issued either in complete chaos and disunity, or in the emergence of an unscrupulous tyrant to whom all that Samuel stood for might well mean nothing. At first humble and devout, "little in his own eyes", Saul ends his career, in spite of Samuel's counsel and support, a proud and rebellious castaway.

It is a second blow to Samuel, and one that he in no way deserved. Though he is stern and forthright in his judgment of the wayward king, yet he grieves deeply for his downfall, and mourns for Saul until God rebukes him. He will not lift his hand against the Lord's anointed. Rather, at Saul's pitiful

request Samuel continues to give the king the public support
and royal courtesies that save his face before the people,
leaving God to remove him from the throne as God sees fit.
The man had let him down, badly and irrevocably, but once
again there is no recrimination, no desertion. Samuel the loyal
stands by the rejected king to the tragic end. If men confuse
this with inconsistency, it is only because they do not understand the nature and the price of loyalty.

For it is only in the context of disagreement, defeat and
rejection that the quality of our fidelity is revealed. It is not
when the policy is happily agreed, and the fellow-workers are
all at one, that loyalty is required, nor when it is our own
leadership that is being followed and our own policy being
pursued. But when our point of view has been rejected, our
warnings disregarded; when the plan being followed is not
what we had wished, then still to pursue with unembittered
spirit and unimpaired zeal the work committed to our hands,
still to share in spiritual fellowship with those who decided
against us, guarding that fellowship with all the greater
vigilance because of the danger of disunity—that is loyalty
indeed.

It is sadly significant of a certain want of character among
many Christian workers, that such an attitude should sometimes
be regar'ed as weak and inconsistent—as though saving our
own face were more important than standing together for the
cause. All allowance must be made for questions of principle,
upon which conscience may demand that we regretfully withhold support. But it remains true that the essence of loyalty
consists not merely in the frank admission that we might after
all be wrong and our colleagues right, but in the recognition
that disagreement and defeat do *not* absolve us from responsibility. We simply must not wash our hands in self-righteous
indignation every time our opinions are rejected. The work,
and the One who called us to it, are greater than we, and
deserve self-effacing fidelity.

It was thus Samuel served Israel in the crisis of her history, disappointed and rejected but faithful still to God, to the people, and to the king; and content to leave his own vindication in the hands of God.

II

Samuel's loyalty found expression not only in his undiminished ministry of counsel, encouragement, warning and legal arbitration, but supremely in his persistent prayer for the nation. When the people finally rejected his advice and repeated their demand for a king he declared, in one of the finest utterances we have from his lips, "God forbid that I should sin against the Lord in ceasing to pray for you". And when he learned that God had rejected Saul and his family from Israel's throne, "Samuel cried unto the Lord all night". We hear nothing at all of the prophet's prayers for himself. The first thing to be noted about the relation between Samuel's fidelity and his prayerfulness is that in him loyalty to God's work and God's people is carried up to the throne of God Himself: fidelity finds its voice in *intercession*.

We have already listened to Abraham praying for Sodom, and have been reminded that Job found release and blessing for his own soul when he prayed for his friends. We might have lingered longer with Moses, and heard his heartfelt cry "Oh this people have sinned a great sin, and have made them gods of gold. Yet now if thou wilt forgive their sin——; and if not, blot me, I pray thee, out of thy book which thou hast written . . ." In such a prayer, not Moses alone but the whole of the Old Testament rises very near to the highest of all intercession, that of Jesus praying for Peter, in the upper room for the eleven, upon the cross for those who crucified Him, and finally "entering heaven with His own blood there to appear in the presence of God for us". We remember the unceasing call in the Apostolic Church for mutual prayer among the members, and with all these instances in mind we can hardly doubt that intercession is prayer at its highest, most wonderful, and most prevailing.

Most wonderful: for in the exercise of intercession we reach the summit of that subtle interpenetration of one spiritual life with others which in the New Testament is called *koinonia*—fellowship—oneness in Christ. In a dozen deep and different ways heart can minister to heart in Christ. We all come to Christ "borne of four", in the sense that others have part in the process that brings us at last face to face, alone, with Christ. And as the roots of our Christian life go back into others' witness and prayer for us, so the branches spread out over other lives; we each cast a shadow of blessing or blight, and "no man liveth unto himself".

Sometimes our emphasis upon individual experience of God's saving grace has obscured this deep truth of the bound-lessness of the spiritual life, and has caused us to overlook the fact that we are far more interdependent than self-sufficient, in the matter of the soul's welfare. In a very real sense we are not simply individuals, in God's sight, but members of a community—or communion—of saints; and wonderful as this truth is at all levels, it passes imagination in its possibilities for good when that communion is translated into mutual inter-cession before the throne of divine grace.

Even at the lowest, most practical estimate mutual inter-cession wields tremendous influence over Christian lives. It *presupposes* so much. When I bring a brother's name before God in my prayer, that brother and I stand pledged together before the throne, linked together in God's sight. I am bound before God to his welfare—to see him henceforth not just as a fellow-Christian whom I happened to meet, but as a sharer with me in the love of Christ, one upon whom I must hence-forth look with Christ's eyes, Christ's sympathy, Christ's understanding.

Mutual intercession, too, on this lower practical level, *prevents* so much. No man who truly prays for me will lightly speak evil of me, or do me harm. To have prayed for a brother imposes a holy restraint upon the tongue, brings an end to quarrels "so far as lieth in us", and dissolves away the smouldering grudges that poison fellowship.

And it *prompts* so much: no one who prays can possibly remain unaware of a brother's need, or unmoved by it. When we pray the answer so often comes in the disturbed conscience and enlightened mind that leads us to fulfil our own requests. Prayer for others leads, more often than not, into determined and sustained effort on their behalf.

But the value of intercession must not be measured in these (so to speak) "by-products". The prayer itself is the greatest service we can render, and in it we reach the utmost limit of our influence for another's good. By our faithful intercession we reach deep within the secret places of another soul, and can get "inside" the enemy lines. By so doing we release divine power that we little dream of, and cannot directly measure. We only know how great it is by considering how barren and futile is a prayerless soul, or for that matter a prayerless Church.

Some faithful souls, it is true, find real difficulty here. They have prayed for years for another's salvation and have not seen the answer. But prayer—we must say again—is not magic, and its influence cannot be wielded outside the will of God, who made all men free. To this important aspect of prayer's limitations, we must return. But meanwhile this much should be said: no one doubts the fearful power of hatred, malice, envy, and ill-will, to hinder, corrupt and infect another soul. Why then should we wonder that goodwill, affection, the earnest desire for another's salvation, lifted in prayer to God for consecration and reinforcement, should achieve so much, even in a life not yet surrendered to divine control? And where the heart for which we pray is already open to heaven's assistance, what new freedom, blessing, power and joy we can impart by praying one for another!

In view of all this, and remembering how we are bound

together in the bonds of Christ, is not failure in the ministry
of intercession a serious symptom of deep disloyalty to the
fellowship of saints?

III

This then is the first thing to be noted about the relation of
Samuel's fidelity to his prayerfulness, that his deep loyalty
found expression in his faithful intercession. The other point
to be noted is that his intercession for the people and for the
king nourished and safeguarded his steadfast fidelity when
otherwise it might have broken. This is much more than mere
playing with words. Spiritual truth is very often two sided,
so that it is difficult to decide which is cause and which effect.
Even so it is with Samuel's character—and in a way Samuel
seems to become more human as we notice it.

Two small but extremely interesting details of the story
deserve attention here. We are told that Israel's demand for a
king "displeased" Samuel, but we are told nothing of the way
in which that displeasure found expression. Nor are we
allowed to hear what Samuel prayed while the displeasure was
still hot within him. But the reply of God is suggestive:
"Hearken unto the voice of the people . . . for they have not
rejected thee, but they have rejected me". Who suggested that
the people had rejected Samuel—if not Samuel himself, in a
prayer of shocked disappointment flowing from a wounded
spirit?

When later Samuel speaks to the people he can bring the
deep assurance "The Lord will not forsake His people for His
great name's sake: because it hath pleased the Lord to make
you a people unto Himself". *Then* he can add, as the consequence of the lesson he himself had learned from the loyalty
of God to His own purposes, "As for me, God forbid that
I should sin against the Lord in ceasing to pray for you".

Does it not all suggest that Samuel's first reaction, as he went
to God with the people's demand, was to pour out his personal

displeasure, and yield to the sharp temptation to give up his task, to resign, to go off in sulks? But as he prayed, the point of view changed, his own personal hurt becomes unimportant beside the challenge offered to God's great name. He learns again that whatever happens God will not give up; that though the people do not deserve it, to cease to pray would be a sin *against the Lord*. And thus in prayer his own loyalty is quickened anew. He returns to the people prepared to try again, and determined to continue in prayer for them, because in God's presence he has realised afresh the patient fidelity of God towards an erring people.

The second detail is of the same kind, and confirms this view of the matter. When Samuel is told of God's judgement upon Saul, we read somewhat surprisingly that "Samuel was wroth". Anger is hardly the emotion we would expect, and the first impression, that Samuel is angry with God, cannot possibly be true. He is very angry with Saul—that is the first reaction. The man who has let him down before the people, in spite of all Samuel had done for him, deserves the scorn and indignation of a great soul. "And Samuel cried unto the Lord all night"—but whether for Saul's reprieve, or in Saul's condemnation, or in deep anguish of spirit at his own disappointment, we are not told. But in the morning the anger is purged away. Samuel conveys God's sentence with a stern and dignified bearing, but repeatedly we are told of Samuel's compassion for the man. Anger against his failure has melted into deep grief for the lost opportunity, and he gives Saul continued public support with an aching heart. "And Samuel mourned for Saul . . . and the Lord said How long wilt thou mourn for Saul seeing I have rejected him . . .?"

There is something very moving about these glimpses of the faithful prophet carrying his wounds, his hot displeasure, his righteous anger, to God Himself in prayer and there finding the truer view of things, the finer spirit, the deeper loyalty which enables him to return to the task without bitterness or

69

cynicism, and to carry on for God. We think not less, but
more of Samuel, when we realise that he too knew those
moments of deep discouragement, and almost of revulsion,
that all Christian workers have felt. Sometimes things we have
worked and prayed for come to nothing; colleagues disappoint
our hopes, betraying our confidence and the cause; the heart
feels lonely and ineffectual, striving to hold clear an unshared
vision, an unwanted truth. The obstacles ahead make further
effort and sacrifice seem a pointless waste. It is probably
true, in spite of all appearance, that the deepest loyalty to God's
work is born in some such spiritual despondency—not in the
flush of success and the thrill of having loyal comrades all
about one, but when in hot displeasure and in anger the heart
turns back to God, only to learn again God's marvellous
patience and unswerving purpose, and in that steadying
Presence to grow calm again.

Samuel's lesson about prayer is not perhaps the most
original, or the most exciting, but many of us in these days
sorely need to learn it. Its inmost meaning, and its value, will
be most apparent to those who are most deeply engaged in the
work of God in difficult situations and discouraging times.
The "Well done" of Christ is given to the *faithful*: *and of that
faithfulness—so Samuel says—intercession for others is at once the
highest expression and the only unfailing source.* God forbid that we
should sin against the Lord in ceasing to pray.

DAVID: THE GOSPEL OF PRAYER

"*Have mercy upon me, O God, according to thy loving kindness: according to the multitude of thy tender mercies blot out my transgressions.
Wash me throughly from mine iniquity, and cleanse me from my sin.
For I acknowledge my transgressions: and my sin is ever before me.
Against thee, thee only, have I sinned, and done that which is evil in thy
sight: . . . Behold, I was shapen in iniquity, and in sin did my mother
conceive me. Behold, thou desirest truth in the inward parts: and in the
hidden part thou shalt make me to know wisdom. Purge me with hyssop,
and I shall be clean: wash me, and I shall be whiter than snow. Make
me to hear joy and gladness . . . Hide thy face from my sins, and blot out
all mine iniquities. Create in me a clean heart, O God; and renew a
right spirit within me. Cast me not away from thy presence; and take
not thy holy spirit from me. Restore unto me the joy of thy salvation:
and uphold me with a free spirit. Then will I teach transgressors thy
ways . . . O Lord, open thou my lips and my mouth shall show forth thy
praise. Thou delightest not in sacrifice; else would I give it: Thou hast
no pleasure in burnt offering. The sacrifices of God are a broken spirit:
a broken and a contrite heart, O God, thou wilt not despise.*"

PSALM 51 (R.V.)

THE OLD TESTAMENT CONTINUALLY SURPRISES US. WE TALK
familiarly about its types and prophecies, its foregleams
and promises, its frequent anticipation of greater
things to come, and we feel we have explained it all as a mere
preparation for the coming of Christ. Then we come upon

71

some sublime passage which seems utterly complete and final in itself, pointing forward to nothing, but expressing its own truth in satisfying form, once for all, leaving nothing more to be said.

The twenty-third Psalm is such a passage: nothing even in the New Testament can add to its beauty or its completeness. As an expression of confidence in God it defies improvement. Micah's great declaration of the requirements of God, Isaiah's magnificent poem on the sovereignty of God, Ezekiel's vision of the life-giving Spirit, are similar "perfect" passages. And high among them, in some respects the most surprising of them, stands David's prayer of penitence, unsurpassed and unparalleled in the whole of Christian literature as the expression of repentance seeking salvation.

In every age, and in every corner of the world, men have found in this Psalm the perfect vehicle of their own confession and the unfailing assurance of God's mercy. One poignant proof of its fitness to express a whole nation's repentance is seen in the addition of verses 18 and 19 to David's original poem, made at a time when Israel returned from Exile to a ruined Jerusalem in chastened and contrite mood. To the Christian mind there may possibly be deeper meanings here and there in David's words than David himself could well have understood, and with Calvary behind us we can offer David's prayer with infinitely greater assurance than he can ever have done. Even so it remains true that Christian piety has produced no finer analysis of contrition, and Christian poetry no more moving exposition of penitence, than this plea of Israel's greatest king for the pardon of the King of Kings.

One might have thought that the New Testament message of a perfected redemption would have evoked some yet more complete and moving prayer for forgiveness, based upon later insights. Yet the nearest prayer in the New Testament, sublime in its own way, but on another level and of a different kind, is the prayer of the publican—"God, be merciful to me, a sinner!" In view of what we are going to discover in this matchless prayer of David, let it be said most definitely at the outset that the publican's prayer is quite sufficient to obtain the mercy it craves. Jesus leaves no shadow of doubt about that. God does not ask of us the elaborate petition and profound analysis of penitence that David gives, before He will show mercy. "God, be merciful to me, a sinner!" is all He requires even of the cleverest soul. But the point that demands attention, and that is of crucial importance in our time, is that the publican's prayer, when uttered from the heart, contains within itself the same penitence of soul that David so powerfully describes.

I

It is necessary to underline this importance, even at the cost of some digression, if the value of this Psalm is fully to be understood. Upon the meaning that we give to repentance turns the inmost truth and power of all evangelical Christianity, and the meaning of the Protestant Reformation. In it lies the moral safeguard and condition of that free grace of God to sinners which *is* the glad tidings of the Gospel, and the central message of all evangelism.

The conditions of divine forgiveness exercised deeply the mind of Martin Luther as he wrestled with the translation of the New Testament and with the abuse of Papal Indulgences, which offered in the Pope's name pardon for sins—at a price. The Church had always required of her converts some evidence of the reality of repentance. The evidence easiest to demand and to measure lay in things like almsgiving, fasting, prayers and self-denial. From this it was an easy step, readily taken by the less thoughtful Christians, to saying that the almsgiving, fasting, prayers and self-denial (under the name of the sacrament of penance) *obtained* forgiveness, and a further easy step to the acceptance of monetary gifts or fines in place of the spiritual disciplines.

This worked out to the great material enrichment of the Church, but to the sad obscuring of the need for penitence, and consequently to the great scandal of the Gospel. Luther saw that penance and true penitence were miles apart. The penitent heart that God requires cannot be pretended, nor substituted by gifts and self-denial, but *must* involve turning with loathing from the sin itself, crying out in broken pride for mercy, and casting oneself by faith upon the grace of Christ. With that realisation Protestantism was born, and New Testament Christianity returned to Europe.

Unfortunately later Protestant Churches have not always followed the reformers in their profound teaching about repentance as the forerunner and condition of faith. The older Puritan theologians perhaps overdid the self-examination, and the spiritual analysis of contrition. But they well knew that the healing balm of forgiveness should be laid only upon a clean wound of penitence if the soul was to regain health. If they went too far and sometimes became excessively intro-spective, the modern Church has not gone nearly far enough. We have largely forgotten the note of personal repentance in modern evangelism.

An illuminating comment has been made upon the experience of the great evangelist of a former generation, D. L. Moody. On his first visit to Britain, we are told, "he needed but to shake the branches of the trees" and the fruit-fall amazed him. On his second visit results were far fewer and in some districts amounted to "scarcely a convert". In correspondence with a great evangelical leader it was suggested that one reason for this was the fact that on his second visit Moody preached much oftener upon the need for repentance towards God, and *the crowds disliked it*.

F. W. Faber has well said that the great want of modern piety is a deep, vigorous, inward repentance, and life goes too fast for that. Rapid livers and rapid thinkers make rapid worshippers, and rapid worshippers are rapid penitents—and the spirit of inward penitence fares ill with all this. Modern ministers know how true that is, and are aware that many doctors and psychiatrists endorse the need for a far deeper and more skilful approach among Christians to the desperate problem of sin, as it weighs—sometimes unsuspected, sometimes even unconsciously—upon modern hearts.

II

Certainly then, an understanding of penitence is important for our evangelism, our teaching, and above all for the depth and purity and spiritual power of our own lives. David's Psalm is undoubtedly the finest introduction to that understanding.

Inevitably Psalm 51 is associated with the darkest sin of David's life, the evil combination of murder, deceit and adultery by which Uriah lost his life, Bathsheba her honour, and David almost his soul. For tyranny, for misuse of responsibility and power, for cowardice, meanness, deceit, lust, ruthless selfishness, injustice and heartlessness the story told in 2 Samuel 11 is hard to beat. The final words, "the thing which David did displeased the Lord" seem an almost frightening understatement of the divine judgement overhanging so vicious a scheme.

For a short while David enjoys the fruit of his sin, but then comes to him Nathan, surely one of Scripture's bravest men, to pronounce the indignation of worthy hearts, and the final judgement of God upon the man David has become. David's pleasure turns to ashes. The whole scheme takes on a new colour in his eyes, and the spiritual consequences begin to weigh intolerably upon his soul. The hateful aftermath of sin —the intense self-loathing, dread of repeated falling, the lost joy, and silenced praise and testimony, the sense of inward corruption—all find eloquent expression in the Psalm. The writer feels the very frame of his being bowed and shattered— his bones crumbling—until out of the deep remorse of a broken

75

man and a broken heart there is born this peerless prayer of penitence.

One thing which the tears of penitence invariably do is to clear the vision, and let the soul see things as they truthfully are. In the new light thrown upon one's conduct, and oneself, all things appear different, not least one's manifold need, and the answer to that need in the nature of God. Even so it is with David's prayer. Broken, changeful, lacking the polished order of a merely literary product, David's poem reads and sounds like the unpremeditated utterance of a heart under deep emotion. Yet it is often thus that deep insight is gained, and David has significant things to say about his sin, God's mercy, the need of renewal, and ground of his hope.

III

The penitent's thought of sin is the only human opinion of it that carries any real weight. David's very vocabulary here is eloquent: he speaks of transgression, of iniquity, and of sin. "Transgression" is the term which isolates the deep rebellion of spirit out of which all evildoing springs. It is the throwing off of the yoke, the spurious demand for a so-called freedom, the proud claim to be exempt from the disciplines and rules that are convenient for other men and for society, but irksome to oneself.

"Iniquity" is a word which lays bare the strange inherent "twist" within the soul, the innate wrongness by reason of which human nature is "buckled" or "warped"—literally, "wrung"—out of true. David realises vividly of what sinful stuff the heart is made. He knows that what has happened is no mere lapse, as a modern might say; no simple accident, for which excuses can be offered; but something inborn, answering all too readily to the outward temptation (the reference to his mother and to his birth conveys this idea in the only way the Hebrew language could do).

And the third term, "Sin", implies David's sense of having missed a mark or goal. It betrays the first awareness of the beginnings of ruin, in that the high and sacred purpose of his life stands fearfully imperilled. The defection of David threatens God's purposes for him and for Israel. Sin *always* involves the defeat of something better God had planned for us.

This is not how David saw his scheme in the hour of hot passion and desire. Then it seemed a splendid opportunity, a simple taking of what all men want and will grasp if they can— and so on. Beforehand, the wrong seems small, and unimportant: afterward, if the heart be not wholly lost, the deed is seen in its enormity. "Transgression" indicts the act of will by which the wrong was deliberately embraced; "iniquity" admits the evil inclination inherent in the nature that could so will; "sin" acknowledges the significance and consequences of what has been done, seen against the background of the divine purpose and goal.

And to this David adds the sharpest confession of all repentant hearts: "Against Thee, Thee only, have I sinned, and done that which is evil in Thy sight". This is no denial that wrong has also been done against Uriah, against Bathsheba, against a child, against a commander in the field, against Israel and the throne. But while the wrong is against many, the sin is against God. Modern men see only the evil done to society, when they take the measure of sin at all. The penitent on his knees knows that without diminishing the significance of wrong done to others, the inmost heart and problem of all wickedness is its direct affront to a holy, and loving, God. In such terms does David sound the first deep note of genuine repentance: "I acknowledge my transgression, and my sin is ever before me . . . against Thee only have I sinned."

IV

The penitent's thought of mercy, too, is alone likely to be adequate to what the sinful heart truly needs. David prays for mercy in three directions. First, for the cancellation of the charge against him, the erasure of the accusing record. Twice he asks that God will "Blot out" the transgression, the iniquity. Such is the request that rises from the sense of guilt, the sharp and bitter knowledge that against one's name and record a shameful thing is rightly, justly, written. He asks that God will obliterate the past. Can it be done? Literally, no. What is written is written, and the true tale can never be untold. But in the grace of God the past can be re-written, with a new meaning. Out of the evil can come forth good, and the remembered sin may be transformed from a festering bitterness that poisons the soul to a humble and thankful testimony to God's mercy, and—as Paul's memory of Stephen—a spur to greater zeal.

David asks, secondly, that God will "wash" him "throughly from iniquity"; "wash me and I shall be whiter than snow". There is some courage in this request, for the word involves a laundering process, the pummelling of soiled clothes, the "treading of the blankets", the kneading of linen at the riverside and wellhead. It is as though David would plead with God to tread, pummell, rough-use his soul until at any cost of humbling and discipline every particle of the stain is washed from the fibres of his personality and the fabric of his life is clean again. The metaphor for sin that likens it to stain dyeing the fabric of the soul occurs again in Isaiah and elsewhere, and corresponds to something very real in spiritual experience. For while God's forgiveness is immediate and free, the removal of sin's stain upon the mind, the imagination, the desire, and even the body, may take time and trouble; it may involve discipline, punishment, sorrow perhaps, as the redeeming Lord "treads white" the hearts that evil has ingrained. But David wants the inmost stain removed.

78

And he asks, thirdly, for another kind of cleansing in addition: "Cleanse me from my sin . . . purge me with hyssop, and I shall be clean". The word used, and the reference to hyssop, set the prayer in the light of the purificatory rites prescribed for the cleansing of the leper, or those contracting uncleanness by contact with the dead, or in other ways. There may also be a distant reference to the Passover Festival and sacrifice, though David makes it clear (verse 16) that he does not think sacrifices can avail for sin like his. The purpose of the "ceremonial" cleansing, as we somewhat lightly call it, was to meet the deep longing of the sinner, which underlay all the sacrificial ritual and every other rite, for acceptance again with God. The convicted heart feels banished, forbidden the Presence, at a distance from God; it knows itself deservedly so, unfitted for acceptance with the Most High. The prayer for this cleansing therefore is the same in content as the cry "Cast me not away from Thy presence . . ."—and once again David surprises us with the depth of his understanding.

Such is the penitent's view of the mercy he needs: a pardon that cancels the just but awful indictment that lies against his soul; an inward purification that shall thoroughly cleanse away the mental and spiritual stain left upon him by the sin; and a restoration to God's presence that shall set him again at one with the eternal holiness and the everlasting love. Truly, a contrite heart attains large views of God's great mercy.

v

The true penitent, however, will not stop at even such deep thoughts of sin, and so uplifting thoughts of mercy. He goes forward with David to think also of the complete renewal of the soul which alone can perfect the work of salvation. Scripture is insistent that redemption deals not merely with our uneasiness about sin, but with sin. Christ came not only to forgive but to free, not only to ransom but to regenerate. The saintly Thomas Shepard, Scottish mystic and founder of Harvard University, cautions that "of all hypocrites we be not evangelical hypocrites", upon which Alexander Whyte comments: "An evangelical hypocrite is a man who sins the more safely because grace abounds; who says to his lusts, both of mind and body, that the blood of Christ cleanseth from all such sin . . ."

The warning is needed, for it is perilously easy to corrupt the Gospel of God's free grace towards sinners into a doctrine of false security or easy escape for the wilfully careless and sinful. David is made acutely aware, in the sharpened self-knowledge of his contrition, that something needs to be done to his nature and his will before his salvation can be complete —or safe.

So David asks for a sixfold renewal: "Thou desirest truth in the inward parts, and in the hidden part thou shalt make me to know wisdom". The mind that could so misjudge the real nature of the deed, that could allow itself to be so blinded by passion and self-will, that could fall into such deception of itself and of others, needed to be reborn into a love of truth and an honesty of thought which should bring both illumination and moral wisdom to bear upon every succeeding temptation.

Behind the darkened, deceived mind lay the train of evil imagination and desire, the wanting of forbidden things, which lends to all temptation its terrible emotive power. Understanding this David cried out, "Create in me a clean heart, O God!"

Once more, since neither thought nor feeling nor both together make up the act of sin, but only the *will*—the acceptance and decision of the whole personality moving towards the accomplishment of the deed—David asks for divine renewal of his inmost selfhood, his essential personality, his "spirit". "Renew a right (steadfast) spirit within me. . . . Take not thy holy spirit from me . . . And uphold me with a free (willing) spirit". Steadfast, holy, willing—Lord keep me so! One senses the deep dread of falling again into folly, and perhaps also the confused realisation of his utter dependence upon One we later learn to know as the Holy Spirit of God, though New Testament thought must not be read into David's phrases. But even without that later revelation, David's prayer has wonderfully analysed the desperate need of the sinful heart which finds its perfect answer in Christ's words to the learned Nicodemus: "Ye must be born again".

Renewal of heart, mind and will must bring renewed *joy*— "Restore unto me the joy of thy salvation . . . make me to hear joy and gladness", for the sin has forfeited David's happiness. In the same way, the sweet singer of Israel has been silenced by his sin, and pleads for a restored *testimony*: "Deliver me from blood-guiltiness, O God, Thou God of my salvation, and my tongue shall sing aloud of Thy righteousness. . . . Open Thou my lips, and my mouth shall show forth Thy praise." So will return also the former *usefulness*, as the "man after God's own heart" can hope once again to influence others towards God: "Then will I teach transgressors Thy ways: and sinners shall be converted unto Thee". No one who has ever knelt at David's stool will wonder that these three things should find place in his prayer—for sin robs us of each, immediately and, unless we find forgiveness, irrevocably.

VI

Conviction, pardon, regeneration: these are the deep notes of true repentance, and the supreme offers of the everlasting Gospel. But one thing more is needful if this prayer of David is to be more than the heart-broken, anguished cry of a laden heart. What ground has David for praying thus? What is his confidence, his hope of being heard? It is not his own earnestness, nor the greatness of his need. Nor is it the promises once made to him when God set him upon the throne—

promises he has forfeited the right to plead. Neither will David make promises to God, of rich libations and endless sacrifices, for he knows that no ritual sacrifice can adequately meet the desperate need of his soul. David pleads no "reasons" why God should ever forgive, and cleanse, and renew a soul so guilty and so defiled—except for the glorious, over-riding, self-sufficient reason of God's great loving-kindness, and the multitude of His tender mercies.

Here are reasons enough, in the character and kindness of our redeeming God, who delighteth in mercy. True, there are conditions, but not such as men had so often imagined (and still imagine)—the labour of one's hands, the heaping of sacrifice upon offering and whole burnt offering. "The sacrifices of God are a broken spirit: a broken and a contrite heart, O God, Thou wilt not despise." That is David's final word, the ground of his prayer, and the foundation of his hope. Beneath all the sorrow and the fears and the humility of David's penitence there yet breathes this note of Gospel assurance, this hope in the loving-kindness of God, in the tender mercy of the Most High, in the will of God to save. That is man's *only* hope.

For David it remained a hope; a strong, well-founded hope, but one nevertheless that fell short of outright, joyous assurance of divine forgiveness. That must await the coming of Jesus, the atonement of the cross, and the gift of the Spirit. But let us not suppose, on that account, that David has nothing to teach us. Our modern habit, already referred to, of treating lightly the need for true repentance, is a serious deficiency of spiritual insight, and dangerously misleading. We assume too readily that because forgiveness is free, it must be easy. We emphasise peace more than purity, comforting rather than cleansing, relief of guilty souls more than regeneration of sinful hearts. Thus would we sometimes heal the hurt of sin too slightly, and evangelical experience and evangelical piety are often shallow in consequence.

Across so many centuries David's prayer still expounds for us unerringly the inner meaning of penitence. *We still need to learn from him the real nature of sin, the sinner's many-sided need of mercy, the depth of that renewal of soul without which even the pardoned life cannot be safe. Equally do we need, with David, to turn away from all other grounds and avenues of hope but the known graciousness of our merciful God.* All is resolved, adjusted, pleaded, and achieved, not through the elaborate machinery of religious organisation and ritual, but in the secret intimacies of personal approach to God. That is David's Gospel of prayer.

SOLOMON: THE HORIZONS OF PRAYER

"*And Solomon stood before the altar of the Lord in the presence of all the congregation of Israel, and spread forth his hands . . . and said, O Lord, the God of Israel, there is no God like Thee, in the heaven or in the earth . . . Hearken Thou to the supplications of thy servant, and of thy people Israel, when they shall pray toward this place: yea, hear thou from thy dwelling place, even from heaven; and when thou hearest, forgive . . . If a man sin against his neighbour, and an oath be laid upon him to cause him to swear, and he come and swear before thine altar in this house . . . And if thy people Israel be smitten down before the enemy . . . When the heaven is shut up and there is no rain . . . If there be in the land famine, if there be pestilence, if there be blasting or mildew, locust or caterpiller; if their enemies besiege them in the land of their cities; whatsoever plague or whatsoever sickness there be . . . Moreover, concerning the stranger, that is not of thy people Israel, when he shall come from a far country for thy great name's sake . . . If thy people go out to battle against their enemies, by whatsoever way thou shalt send them . . . If they sin against thee . . . and thou be angry with them, and deliver them to the enemy, so that they carry them away captive unto a land far off or near; yet if they shall bethink themselves in the land whither they are carried captive, and turn again . . . then hear thou from heaven, and maintain their cause; and forgive thy people which have sinned against thee . . . Now when Solomon had made an end of praying, the fire came down from heaven, and consumed the burnt offering and the sacrifices; and the glory of the Lord filled the Lord's house.*"

2 CHRONICLES 6: 12–39; 7: 1 (R.V.)

84

SOLOMON: THE HORIZONS OF PRAYER

FEW WOULD COUNT SOLOMON AMONG THE MEN OF PRAYER; he is, at any rate, hardly one who might be held up as an example of what it means to live by prayer, or of what prayer can accomplish. His life, like Saul's, was from a religious point of view a disastrous disappointment. In Solomon's case the glory of his other successes, which were magnificent, only throws into sharper relief the failure of his character and obedience. Nevertheless we shall include Solomon in our studies for the sake of his long recorded prayer, because it is a type of prayer found hardly anywhere else in the Bible—the formal, national, ceremonial prayer of a King in the presence of his people on a great State occasion. Indeed there is something rather grandiose about the great bronze pulpit, and the kneeling figure with widespread hands intoning the eloquent introduction and carefully balanced sonorous paragraphs: we are irresistibly reminded of "Solomon in all his glory".

Nevertheless Solomon's prayer has in one respect a very special significance which demands attention. It is a prayer with very wide horizons. Most of the prayers so far studied have been personal and private; except for Abraham's and Samuel's, personal in aim; all of them private in expression. Some earnest folk argue that all prayer is necessarily private, and intimate, but that is manifestly untrue. The Master sharply reminds us that public prayer which is merely a showing-off of piety "to be seen of men" is no true prayer—the notice of men is all the answer it will get. But our Lord left no doubt upon the minds of His disciples that there was place also, and large place, for prayer that is not merely private devotion, or personal supplication.

It may seem harsh to say that prayer can become intensely selfish, self-concerned and self-offered. Perhaps the prayer-life begins for most people in the urgent personal cry "God, be merciful to me . . . Lord, bless me, even me". But we cannot remain there, we must lift our eyes to wider horizons

85

if anything like the depth and height of prayer-experience is to become ours. Wherever they might have begun, it is probably true to say that the great exponents of prayer have come at length rarely to pray for themselves—though they would ever acknowledge their need to do so. In spite of his disappointing career, Solomon does profitably remind us that the prayer-life stimulates a great breadth of outlook.

I

Very surprisingly, this solemn occasion of the dedication of Solomon's Temple seems to be the nearest approach we have in the Old Testament to a prayer-meeting. Certainly, it does not look like a prayer-meeting, but equally certainly we have the nation gathered for prayer, being led in supplication by one representing all, and in all probability joining together in the repeated words "Hear thou from thy dwelling place, even from heaven; and when thou hearest, forgive", as a liturgical refrain or response. This is one of several touches that make one wonder if Solomon's prayer was composed for the great occasion by one of the priests.

If, indeed, we may regard the assembly as a meeting for united prayer, we must confess that the opportunity was largely lost in the way that such occasions are so very frequently spoiled: by one person monopolising the prayertime and asking all there is to ask. And by far too much direction as to what other people should pray for! But there is no need to press the argument. We simply accept the suggestion that as Samuel reminded us of the duty of praying *for* one another, Solomon may remind us of the equally urgent duty of praying *with* one another.

The prayer-meeting is in truth one of the enrichments of spiritual life which we owe to the New Testament, to its message of the "new and living way into the holiest of all", its truth of the priesthood of all believers, and its wonderful new fellowship in the Body of Christ. It is a creation of the new covenant, though hardly appreciated as such by the majority of present-day Christians. The clear promise of our Lord, that where two or three gather in His name (the preceding verse makes clear that one purpose of the gathering is for prayer) there He is in the midst of them; and the assurance that if two agree touching anything that they shall ask it shall be done, ought to invest every assembly of Christians for common prayer with a unique excitement and expectancy.

The curious ten days of "idleness", when heaven and earth waited and the agelong purpose of God seemed to halt, take on a wholly new significance when we realise that God was waiting for the Church to be *ready* for Pentecost. He was waiting, in fact, for the Church to be found with one accord in one place at prayer. Renewed fellowship in prayer brought a repeated Pentecost, when the place was shaken where they were assembled, and great boldness came upon all. A similar result followed when prayer was made without ceasing of the Church unto God for the imprisoned Peter. The prayer movement of 1784, the experience of the 1904 awakening in Wales, and the testimony of Dr. Graham in our own time, all confirm the suspicion that the modern Church has very much to learn about a whole "fourth dimension" of corporate life and power. It is the range of spiritual experience and achievement only comprehensible to those who have learned the astonishing stimulation of corporate prayer.

Prayer in fellowship with others is not learned swiftly or automatically. It imposes its own discipline upon thought and feeling, the subordination of oneself and one's own petitions to the common seeking. At the same time it liberates the spirit, opening up spheres of intercession and a freedom in supplication before unknown. Before a service it creates the atmosphere of freedom, expectancy and readiness which is so essential to the fruitful preaching of the Word, and in these days so rare. Christian workers labour together more easily, argue together

87

more amicably, rejoice together more frequently, when they are each determined that nothing shall prevent their praying together. In spite of all this, many modern Christians live upon the Old Testament level in this respect, and are island-bound in private prayer. Solomon rebukes this isolation and flings wide the *horizon of prayer-fellowship* to include Israel in his act of supplication.

II

Solomon's petition reveals surprising breadth of mind in a second way, at least equally worthy of careful notice, in the wide horizon of his large and farseeing requests. The occasion, the dedication of the Temple, was the climax of months and years of strenuous preparation. It was a truly great moment for king and nation. Yet it was fraught with its dangers.

The real dedication of a sacred place lies not in the stones, the site, or the fabric. It lies in the attitude of the worshippers to it, in the place which the shrine comes to occupy in the affection and thought and loyalty of those who use it. So Solomon prays that Israel will come to think reverently of the new Temple, and act reverently towards it. It is hard to transfer affection from the old site of worship and blessing to some new one; and Israel had memories of the Ark of God resting first at Shiloh in Samuel's great days, and then at Kirjath Jearim. Nothing could effect the change, in the heart of the people, but experience of such blessing, and the up-building of such habits of reverence, in respect of the *new* building, that the memories of the *old* would be eclipsed.

If this did not happen, the labour and magnificence en-shrined in the new sanctuary would be but empty mockery of its unsanctified uselessness, monument of a generation whose real religion was buried beneath walls of cedar, and altars of brass and graven work of fine gold. With very good reason did Solomon plead that the new Temple might come to possess such sacred associations in the mind and memory of

88

the people, that it might become truly the house of God to the nation, the silent witness to the supremacy of God's will in the · nation's affairs. And as he develops this theme in prayer, his thought and petition range widely over the nation's life, and forwards through the future years.

After a somewhat elaborate preamble, in which Solomon is mainly concerned about the continuance of his own dynasty, he makes his first request for the Temple, that God's "eyes may be open day and night, even towards the place whereof thou hast said that thou wouldest put thy name there; to hearken unto the prayer which thy servant shall pray toward this place. And hearken thou to the supplications of thy servant, and of thy people Israel, when they shall pray toward this place . . ."

He asks, that is to say, that the new Temple shall become in the faith and memory of Israel the place of answered prayer. He pleads that it shall be hallowed by many occasions when God heard the cry of His people, and answered their plea— sometimes in the night watches, when the sleepless sick turn their faces towards the shrine, or those who keep anxious vigil make their prayer facing Jerusalem; sometimes in the day- time when the burden is heavy and the duty unpleasant or exhausting. Nothing can sanctify a place or an occasion, like the vivid memory of answered prayer and granted blessing. If in Israel's heart, or ours, the place of worship proves the place where God heard our prayer and saw our tears, it needs no other hallowing. It is the first thing we might ask for all our Churches.

The king's second request is that the Temple might become so sacred in the eyes of the people that oaths made in its precincts will be binding upon the conscience in the sight of God. This is quite a crucial matter. We are back in the days when inability to read or write, or sign documents, meant that trade, contracts and public affairs depend almost entirely upon the truth of one's word, the integrity behind a promise. It may seem a strange kind of religious faith that is prepared to lie, to steal or swindle, but not before the altar, not upon consecrated ground, not with the hand upon the Bible. Nevertheless upon the sacredness of the oath the most solemn human relationships rested for many centuries.

Here will lie one of the sure tests of the place the new Temple holds in the thought of the people. Will it become the safeguard of the honesty of business, the integrity of human relationships, the justice of man's dealing with man? Will the Temple worship prove the spring and guardian of social righteousness and public morality? Again we think of our own centres of worship—and know what we should pray concerning their influence in the life of our nation.

Next, Solomon asks that the new Temple might become the place of renewal for those who are defeated. "And if thy people Israel be smitten down before the enemy, because they have sinned against thee; and shall turn again, and confess thy name, and pray and make supplication before thee in this house: then hear thou from heaven, and forgive the sin of thy people Israel, and bring them again into the land which thou gavest to them and to their fathers."

Too often in failure and defeat the heart turns away from the house of God, nursing its wounds with bitterness and complaint, prolonging its ordeal by deserting the very place where victory might be gained. In the end we have always to return there, with confession, and contrite pleading for power to fight again. Solomon asks that the nation might learn, early and well, that in God's presence the pierced armour may be replaced, the broken sword repaired, the daunted heart once more made strong.

Sometimes defeat is easier to bear than drought, when the land (or the soul) lies parched and barren, beside the great desert, under rainless skies. "When the heaven is shut up, and there is no rain, because they have sinned against thee; if they pray toward this place, and confess thy name, and turn from their sin, when thou dost afflict them: then hear thou in heaven, and forgive the sin of thy servants, and of thy people Israel, when thou teachest them the good way wherein they should walk; and send rain upon thy land, which thou hast given to thy people for an inheritance." There is a whole philosophy of spiritual drought in the phrases of that petition—its causes, its discipline and its cure, as the king pleads that God will make the Temple a fountain of refreshment for the thirsty soul.

And a place of refuge in the day of private or public calamity. Whenever famine, pestilence, blasting or mildew, locust or caterpillars, siege or plague, or whatsoever sickness (and every man shall know his own plague and his own sorrow) shall fall upon Israel, and men turn in distress to spread their hands in anguished pleading towards "this house"—then begs Solomon, "hear thou from heaven thy dwelling place, and forgive, and render unto every man according to all his ways, whose heart thou knowest; (for thou, even thou only, knowest the hearts of the children of men;) that they may fear thee, to walk in thy ways, so long as they live in the land which thou gavest unto our fathers."

It is worthy of remark that the king seeks no mere favours, no immunity of Israel from sorrow and affliction. God's knowledge of the heart and its frequent need of humbling must decide what Israel's experience shall be. But Solomon asks that as the long years pass the Temple may become the place to which increasingly the heart of Israel under corrective affliction may instinctively turn—not only for comfort and for healing, but for teaching too, that the meaning of the experience may not be missed.

The sixth petition is probably the most unexpected, as it is certainly the broadest in its vision. "Moreover concerning the stranger, that is not of thy people Israel, when he shall come from a far country for thy great name's sake, and thy mighty hand, and thy stretched-out arm; when they shall come and pray toward this house: then hear thou from heaven, even from thy dwelling place, and do according to all that the stranger calleth to thee for; that all the peoples of the earth may know thy name, and fear thee, as doth thy people Israel, and that they may know that this house which I have built is called by thy name."

Often and again Israel forgot the world-vision implied in the convenant with Abraham, that "in thee and in thy seed shall all the nations of the earth be blessed". It is thus the more significant that Solomon's Temple should express not only hospitality for the alien and the stranger, but something of the world-purpose inherent in the divine election of Israel. Herod's Temple, which succeeded Solomon's, contained a "court of the Gentiles". It is some measure of the importance Jesus attached to it, that (according to Mark's account) at the Messianic cleansing of the Temple, He quoted the words of Isaiah, "My house shall be called a house of prayer for all the nations . . ." and drove from this "court of the Gentiles" those who for private profit had denied its use to the stranger and foreigner. It must be admitted that Solomon's breadth of vision here may have had something to do with his pride in the far-flung empire that he ruled. Even so, we may profit by his example and take care that the boundaries of our prayer-life remain as wide as the purposes of God.

The seventh petition in this remarkable prayer requests that the new Temple may become the place from which Israel shall set out upon great and successful enterprises, to wage victorious campaigns "as God wills". "If thy people go out to battle against their enemies, by whatsoever way thou shalt send them, and they pray unto thee toward this city which thou hast chosen, and the house which I have built for thy name; then hear thou from heaven their prayer and their supplication, and maintain their cause."

The battle must be that to which God shall send, if the issue is to be successful. And the prayer for God's help must be sincere. Far too often public prayer in time of war has forgotten that God must defend *the right*. But when the heart is set upon the will of God, then the place of prayer becomes the spring from which great undertakings flow. The moment of worship becomes the moment of commissioning to new and wider campaigning for the King. Looking ahead to the years of Israel's glorious destiny, Solomon asks that future expansion shall all begin at the house of God.

The final prayer is so amazingly appropriate to the circumstances of the Exile, four centuries later, that we must assume either that it was added long afterwards, or that Solomon possessed profound foresight of the trend of events in Israel. "If they sin against thee (for there is no man that sinneth not), and thou be angry with them, and deliver them to the enemy, so that they carry them away captive unto a land far off or near; yet if they shall bethink themselves in the land whither they are carried captive, and turn again, and make supplication unto thee in the land of their captivity, saying, We have sinned . . . if they return unto thee with all their heart and with all their soul . . . and pray toward their land, which thou gavest unto their fathers, and the city which thou hast chosen, and toward the house which I have built for thy name: then hear thou from heaven, even from thy dwelling-place, their prayer and their supplications, and maintain their cause, and forgive thy people which have sinned against thee."

Once more we are surprised at the breadth of sympathy expressed in this prayer. In the confidence that God will not cast off his people, but will have compassion upon His banished ones, the king pleads that the House of God in the homeland shall remain the spiritual home of the distant exile and backslider—and the place of his final return.

III

The prayer is long, because the requests are for big things. We can ask no greater things for the Churches of our own land, and the shrines where we ourselves worship, than that each should become through God's blessing, a place of answered prayer, a guardian of morality, a haven of renewal for the defeated, refreshment for the parched, refuge for the afflicted, a spiritual home for the stranger, the starting-point of great undertakings, and the place of return for the backslider and the exile. That so long ago a king of Israel should ask just this for the house of prayer that he had built, shows a breadth of vision and an understanding of the wider ranges of prayer that is equally impressive, whether we think the king himself penned its phrases, or the priests who had so much to do with the record of his reign.

"Thou art coming to a King, large petitions with thee bring" is the prayer counsel of John Newton, though the prayer from which the quotation comes does not move outside the inward needs of the individual life. How often that is true of earnest souls! "With my burden I begin"—and frequently end, not only in the sense that we get no farther, but in the sense that we find prayer dull and unrewarding, and slowly cease to pray. Let another king—admirable in few things but certainly right in this—*teach us to lift the horizons of prayer to include our fellows in the shared act of prayer, and to range far and wide over earth and time in the things we ask.* "For His grace and power are such, none can ever ask too much."

ASA: THE INSIGHTS OF PRAYER

"And Asa had an army that bare bucklers and spears, out of Judah three hundred thousand; and out of Benjamin, that bare shields and drew bows, two hundred and fourscore thousand: all these were mighty men of valour. And there came out against them Zerah the Ethiopian with an army of a thousand thousand, and three hundred chariots; and he came unto Mareshah. And Asa cried unto the Lord his God, and said, Lord, there is none beside thee to help, between the mighty and him that hath no strength: help us, O Lord our God; for we rely on thee, and in thy name are we come against this multitude. O Lord, thou art our God; let not man prevail against thee. So the Lord smote the Ethiopians before Asa, and before Judah; and the Ethiopians fled."

2 CHRONICLES 14: 8–12

THE STORY OF ASA, KING OF JUDAH, PROVIDES A FAIR illustration of the deep difference of viewpoint that divides the politician and the priest, when they are considering not only the same period of history and the same person, but even the same event and deed.

According to what may be called the royalist, or political, record in 1 Kings 15, Asa was an astute diplomat, not above intrigue, knowing the power of wealth and the price of his enemies. His religious and moral reforms may have been sincere, but they also served greatly to strengthen his position. While his recovery of the treasures of the Temple is recorded

95

as a religious act, it is immediately added that he knew how
and when to use those same treasures for scarcely religious
ends. Faced with an alliance between the northern kingdom,
Israel, and Benhadad of Syria, and with dangerous forti-
fications on his northern frontier prepared for assault, Asa
bribed Benhadad to desert the alliance, and by attacking Israel
to relieve the threat to Judah. The scheme succeeded. The
aggressive fortress was dismantled, and the record closes with
the suggestion of the king's prosperity and power. The
impoverishment of the Temple was apparently accepted as no
great price to pay for security.

On the other hand the religious, or priestly record in
2 Chronicles, is not nearly so satisfied with Asa's reign. His
reforms are mentioned, and a sincere piety is attributed to
his early years. Much more is made of a revival of the ancient
Covenant between Israel and God, under the prompting and
warning of a prophet called Azariah son of Oded—a "revival"
carried through under penalty of death by the sword!

The successful intrigue with Benhadad is also mentioned,
but this time a prophet, Hanani the seer, sternly rebukes Asa
both for the method and for the implications of this deed:
"Because thou hast relied on the king of Syria, and hast not
relied on the Lord thy God . . . Herein hast thou done
foolishly". "Then Asa was wroth with the seer, and put him
in the prison house; for he was in a rage with him because of
this thing. And Asa oppressed some of the people at the same
time". The last statement is somewhat irrelevant just here,
and seems to be added to avoid the impression that the priestly
historian was antagonistic merely on account of the loss of the
Temple treasures, or the imprisonment of a prophet!

The total impression we are given of Asa is therefore
ambiguous and uncertain. Perhaps the Chronicler's phrase,
"the acts of Asa, first and last," is meant to suggest some
serious inconsistency between his earlier life and his latter
years. If this is so, the difference between early profession

and later performance may explain the unexpected sharpness of Hanani's rebuke. At the battle with Ethiopia Asa had prayed "Help us O Lord our God; for we rely on thee . . ." Now, after the subterfuge with Syria, Hanani says "Were not the Ethiopians . . . a huge host, with chariots and horsemen exceeding many? yet, because thou didst rely on the Lord, he delivered them into thy hand . . . Because thou hast relied on the king of Syria, and hast not relied on the Lord thy God, therefore is the host of the king of Syria escaped out of thy hand." Even prophets do not usually reproach a man in the very words of his own former prayer. The Chronicler himself appears to underline the point again when he adds, a little unsympathetically, that "Asa was diseased in his feet; his disease was exceeding great: yet in his disease he sought not to the Lord, but to the physicians".

Whatever the politicians thought of Asa, therefore, the priestly verdict on his reign is brief and pointed: "disappointing—a failure in faith."

I

It is not therefore to Asa's personal example that we look for a lesson on prayer, but rather to the one feature of his earlier petition which was so remembered by his contemporaries, and by his later critic. This is the moving phrase which expresses perfectly his simple and complete reliance upon the supreme power of God, in all circumstances and against all odds. It affirms his confidence that when God's help is at hand, all weighing of circumstances, all calculation of opposing forces, and estimating of probable results, is wholly out of place. The resources of the enemy, in Asa's eyes, matter nothing compared to the resources of prayer.

Unfortunately the impressive words of the Authorised Version—"Lord, it is nothing with thee to help, whether with many, or with them that have no power: help us O Lord our God, for we rest on thee . . ."—may not pass unchallenged.

97

The Revised Version gives, "Lord, there is none beside thee to help, between the mighty and him that hath no strength . . ." which apparently means, there is none to compare with God for helping the "little man". But the Revised margin alters to "There is no difference with thee to help, whether the mighty or him that hath no strength". The usually excellent Revised Standard Version tries again with "O Lord there is none like thee to help, between the mighty and the weak"—which sounds much better until we ask what is meant by "between".

In the multitude of translations there is much confusion! We are obviously wrestling here with the unfitness of the comparatively simple and uncomplicated Hebrew language to express a fairly complicated idea. But as so often is the case, the idea is plain in all renderings: when God intervenes to help, human strength or weakness matter nothing. The calculation of material resources and prospects becomes irrelevant. If God be for us, who is he—whoever he may be—that is against us?

Ethiopia's two-to-one preponderance, the hopeless situation, the three hundred chariots—(an overwhelming superiority in arms which could evoke panic in Judah)—and the enemy's first choice of battle-ground: these add up to imminent and crushing defeat, by all military and natural precedents. Against them all, the help of God suffices. Asa's rallying call, "Thou art our God, we rely on thee, let not man prevail against thee . . ." is long remembered whenever the story of that day's victory is told. It is nothing with God to help, whether with many or with them that have no power.

The cynic declares that God is on the side of the big battalions, and prospers them that have the forces. The insight of Asa, which is the characteristic insight of all praying hearts, sees that when God is on the field numbers cease to count: there is nothing too difficult for the Lord of hosts.

We should not miss the point that Asa musters all his forces, nevertheless; and a splendid array they make. Judah had produced no such army hitherto. Asa knows that God's miracles are not wrought for the shiftless and unconcerned. But when all our best is in the battle, when we are committed to the last ounce of our strength, and striving mightily— "in God's name"—then the great multitude must give way, and the terrifying odds against us dwindle. Their horses are but flesh, and mortal man cannot prevail against his Maker. This is the faith that came to Asa in the hour of his earnest intercession; whatever happened afterwards, we ought not to miss his contribution to the rich teaching of the Bible on the meaning and value of prayer.

II

Not that Asa is alone in this testimony. The Bible says in many ways what Asa expressed in his memorable words. Jonathan declared it to his armour-bearer as they went up against the Philistines: "There is no restraint with the Lord to save by many or by few". The two undaunted spies said it to all Israel, when the ten counselled retreat: "Let us go up at once and possess the land; for we are well able to overcome it . . . If the Lord delight in us, then he will bring us into this land . . . neither fear ye the people of the land; for they are bread for us: their defence is departed from them, and the Lord is with us: fear them not."

Gideon's three hundred declare it again as they surround the hosts of Midian. Elisha prays that God will open his young servant's eyes to see the ranks of divine horsemen round about God's man, working, watching, silent and unseen, but always there, outnumbering all enemies. And on a deeper, immensely more significant level, Jesus speaks of it in Gethsemane, "Thinkest thou that I cannot now pray to my Father, and he shall presently give me more than twelve legions of angels?"— though for His divine work's sake He will not accept that deliverance. Always the resources are there: with God the little one becomes a thousand, and a Babe shall break an empire.

III

There lies behind this insight a profound and far-reaching faith, and there issues from it an equally profound and far-reaching principle, both eloquently illustrated in Scripture.

The faith finds perhaps its finest expression in the ancient song of Deborah. Here, as so often, Israel is at war with a vastly superior enemy. She is divided and incomplete, ten thousand is the total of her army, with not a spear or shield among them. Sisera, leader of the Canaanites has nine hundred chariots of iron! Yet out of the bitter and unequal struggle Israel won through to freedom and a great destiny. Deborah celebrates the victory in a taunt song of great power. When men and allies and weapons were few, and trusted friends proved false, then Israel found higher sources of help and deliverance, "the stars in their courses fought against Sisera"; the ancient river Kishon helped to drown the foe, heaven and earth conspired with Israel, the universe was on her side, because the Lord Jehovah Himself marched at their head.

Here in ancient poetic terms is the fundamental truth of all religion, the basic faith of humanity, that the universe is on the side of right—that the man who is in the right has God and the universe behind him, while the man who is in the wrong, whatever seeming advantages he may have, has set his course against the eternal current of things. Sooner or later that current will tell against him. There may be in the saying something of superstition as well as of poetry, but the truth at the heart of it is the same as that which philosophers teach when they speak of our living "in a moral universe". It is the same truth that the Old Testament prophets declare when they insist that Jehovah is the King, Lawgiver and Judge of all the earth. It is the same truth that Paul expresses in the famous words about all things working together to promote goodness.

This faith implies that in the universe, and in history, there is *a certain moral logic of events*, which ensures that in the long run only goodness yields any permanent profit, only truth endures, while evil and error have within themselves the seeds of their own decay.

It means, too, that there is in the universe and in history *a deep purpose of good*—that the world is not indifferent to man's struggles. Nature yields up her secrets to those who love truth, and life yields up her joys to those who love virtue. Every honest endeavour to do God's will, every earnest struggle to rise nearer to God's ideal for men, has the current of God's purpose behind it, bearing the believing soul surely onward to the one-far-off divine event towards which the whole creation moves.

And it means, in consequence, that there are in the universe and in history *powers available to the prayerful spirit*, that ensure that truth and goodness shall not be defeated. The race is not to the merely swift, nor the battle to the merely strong. Forces of evil, however cunning and well armed, must ever fail against those higher energies of virtue and of God that prayer can command. Admittedly this seems a very large faith to find in so ancient and so brief a text about the stars in their courses —but it is there: and it is the deep faith behind Asa's confidence that Ethiopia's vast numbers are unimportant if God be on Israel's side.

IV

For the best illustration of the equally deep and far-reaching principle of Christian service, which we said issues from this insight of Asa's about the power of God and material forces, we must turn to the New Testament; to Paul's penetrating discovery in the hour of his weakness and frustration. He writes to the Corinthians about his repeated prayer that God would remove the thorn in his flesh, the messenger of Satan by which he was buffetted, and his work for God—apparently —hindered. The prayer is not granted, but grace is promised.

More important, God lets Paul understand the secret of the experience. The abundance of the revelations given to Paul might easily exalt him above measure, making him proud

THEY TEACH US TO PRAY

and unusable in God's hands. Paul discovers that in enforced weakness he is stronger than in health—stronger, that is, because he is kept dependent on divine wisdom, strength and grace. When I am weak, he says, then am I strong; God's strength is made perfect in weakness. Most gladly therefore will I rather glory in my infirmity.

This but carries Asa's word to its logical conclusion. It is nothing to God—this calculation of human resources and material strength. His power has other sources, other instruments, other levels of operation. He is seen most obviously at work in the weakest of his servants, provided only that they be faithful. Where the situation looks most hopeless, He best shows His hand. So to count upon this as to rejoice in adversity and opposition, is to show Asa's faith at its highest and to have learned once and for all that the divine resources available to prayer are of another order, and another magnitude, than any that human estimates can measure.

v

St. Francis of Assisi was head of a very little band of consecrated men, scorned by former friends, misunderstood by many, opposed by some, even within his beloved Church. Perplexed about the future, he withdrew from his equally perplexed and downhearted followers for a whole silent night. He returned with the dawn to bid them be of good cheer, "for he had seen all the roads crowded with men, French, German, English, running to give themselves to the divine obedience." It was no idle dream, but the beginning of such a revival of infectious and rejoicing religion as Europe has hardly seen. Here was another soul who had called earnestly upon God and had seen, with the deep insight of prayer, that it is nothing with God to save by many or by few, by those that are strong or by those that have no power. *For all power belongeth unto God*: that is Asa's heartening message to all who do not always pray, and do faint.

ELIJAH: THE JUDGEMENTS OF PRAYER

"*Elias was a man subject to like passions as we are, and he prayed earnestly that it might not rain: and it rained not on the earth by the space of three years and six months. And he prayed again, and the heaven gave rain, and the earth brought forth her fruit . . . And it came to pass at the time of the offering of the evening sacrifice, that Elijah the prophet came near, and said, Lord God of Abraham, of Isaac and of Israel, let it be known this day that thou art God in Israel, and that I am thy servant . . . Then the fire of the Lord fell, and consumed the burnt sacrifice, and the wood, and the stones, and the dust, and licked up the water that was in the trench. And when all the people saw it they fell on their faces: and they said, The Lord, he is the God; the Lord, he is the God . . . And Elijah arose, and went for his life . . . and came and sat down under a juniper tree: and requested for himself that he might die; and said, It is enough; now, O Lord, take away my life; for I am not better than my fathers . . . And he arose and . . . went into Horeb, the mount of God. . . .*"

JAMES 5: 17, 18; 1 KINGS 18: 36–39; 19: 3–8

THE EXAMPLE WHICH THE APOSTLE JAMES CHOOSES TO illustrate his statement that "the supplication of a righteous man availeth much in its working"—the example of Elijah—is highly significant, if a little unexpected. It serves well as a further reminder (if such could still be needed) that prayer is not by any means the mere escape of

103

the defeated, the refuge only of the weak and the frustrated; it is, too, the strength of the mighty, and the weapon of the warrior.

Elijah is essentially a warrior-prophet, campaigning for justice against oppression (as in the moving story of Naboth and his vineyard), for Israel against Ahab, her would-be tyrant king, and for God against the Baal-spirits when Israel "halts between two opinions". And his mightiest weapon is prayer. First, the prayer of judgement that inaugurated the drought which was to bring Israel to her knees. Then, on Carmel, the prayer of witness that called upon God to vindicate His name, and brought down fire upon the thrice-drenched sacrifice.

Ahab, the prophets of Baal, and all Israel with them tremble before this Tishbite with the rough clothes and plain manners of the desert places. But it is not his rebuke, nor his warnings, that strike awe into their hearts, but the certainty that God stands behind him to hear his prayer, for them and against them, and to uphold his word. Elijah's is the prayer of courage, of power, of assault upon the Lord's enemies, prayer wielded as an instrument of spiritual warfare. And like all true prayer it is "of a piece" with the character of the man, rugged, aggressive, uncompromising. This is what impressed James (and the Jewish teachers from whom he is probably borrowing his thought): the combination of strong passions, disciplined in a powerful nature, consecrated to the Lord's cause, and issuing in strong, effective and prevailing prayer. Outwardly, as Israel and Ahab saw him, Elijah is a man whose praying is to be feared. His prayer is the prayer of judgement.

I

There is, however, another side to Elijah's prayer experience, one from which we may learn more that fits our personal situation than we do from his use of prayer as a weapon in his unique, prophetic ministry. With Israel, we stand in awe of Elijah on Mount Carmel. But we sit nearer to him, sympathise more deeply with him, in the black mood that fell upon him under the juniper tree. There is a strain of pessimism in many of us, and the more zealous we are for God's work, the more likely it is that we have known moments when, like Elijah, we have felt that all is failure and frustration, the ideal impossible, and the future without hope.

Moreover we can recognise clearly the various symptoms of Elijah's trouble. There is reaction, for one thing, after the brilliant triumph on Mount Carmel. He has demonstrated with dramatic finality that Jehovah is God in Israel. The people have declared their conviction, the priests of Baal have been destroyed, and Ahab has been defeated. In a tremendous victory for truth and for God, Elijah has towered above all Israel in the splendour of his faith and daring. But reaction sets in as soon as the people disperse, and a threatening message from Jezebel is sufficient to send his spirit swinging to the far extreme—from fighting to fear, from defiance to flight.

There is nothing unusual about that. We should all be much safer, and suffer fewer extremes of feeling, if we had the wisdom and self-knowledge to *expect* reaction after any great moment in spiritual experience. It is natural; partly a matter of nervous energies temporarily exhausted; partly a necessary deflating of emotions too strong to be sustained; partly too, simple disappointment that the great moment has passed and we must return to normal. But unrecognised it can be crushing, and dangerous.

There is too the tendency to self-accusation. There seems no good reason why Elijah should say "I am no better than my fathers"—no reason, that is, except that self-disparagement is an invariable symptom of this mood of spiritual despondency. The keenly conscientious do sometimes blame themselves for quite unnecessary misgivings, and charge themselves with omissions and failures that no one else would lay to their door.

The despondency in this way becomes a vicious circle, and the mood feeds upon itself.

We may notice at the same time the familiar tendency to harp on one theme—always present in our dejected, self-pitying moods. Twice the question comes to Elijah, "What doest thou here?" implying he had no business there. And Elijah has a stock answer, "I have been very jealous for the Lord, the God of hosts; for the children of Israel have forsaken thy covenant, thrown down thine altars, and slain thy prophets with the sword; and I, even I only, am left; and they seek my life to take it away"—twice repeated, word for word. It matters nothing that the recital is a little inaccurate: he knows his grievance by heart. We are never very bright mentally, nor very logical, when we are downcast.

Equally typical of these moods is the deep pessimism that sees no ray of hope for the future. "I, I only, am left". He sees the picture in its very worst colours, exaggerating the evil in the situation, wholly omitting to assess the effects of Carmel's crucial result, and leaving God Himself out of the reckoning. "It is enough" he says, which is but an elegant way of saying he is thoroughly "fed-up", downcast, dejected, despairing, and desiring to die. Few of us can claim we have never known something of that blackest of moods; we recognise the symptoms only too well.

II

There is of course something of sin about such a state of soul. But what matters even more than its correct diagnosis, is its cure. What do you do about it? Elijah poured out his complaint to God, and while complaining is never noble, at least it comes nearest to nobility when a man turns his disappointment and despondency, not to his neighbour, or inwards upon himself, but upwards to his God. Then at last he is sincerely seeking the way out.

Elijah went off to Horeb, better known as Sinai. It was a desert place, rugged and wild, where something of nature's own ministry of healing could soothe his spirit. It was solitary, too, and solitude has power to heal the wounds we receive amid the throngs of competing men. But far more significantly, it was the Mount of God. On those wild slopes Elijah could stand again where Moses had communed with God at the burning bush, could imagine if he wished the echo of that Voice which had thundered forth the sacred Law, could take shelter beside the rock whence had gushed forth water under the rod of Moses, could ponder (and it would seem from his words that he did so) the ancient covenant of God with Israel, sealed at the foot of this very mountain. Every spot, every scene on Horeb was hallowed to Israel by old associations with the nation's hero and the nation's God. It was the first trysting place of Jehovah and His people. Elijah went to Horeb because God was wont to be found there.

And this is no mere parable. It is a poor, and vulnerable life that has no Horeb, no place of solitude, and memories; no inner shrine where we have hitherto found God, but only roads and market-places, bazaars and temples, where all too often God is lost sight of, or crowded out. For in fleeing to Horeb, Elijah was obeying the true spiritual instinct that turns *outwards* from the soul's self-obsessing mood, *outwards* from the black depression, *outwards* from the self-pity, and the jaundiced assessment of things. He was seeking those things that are external to ourselves, that rest not upon our feelings and beliefs, but are fixed, constant, unchanging and cannot be erased. Moses and the Law, the Exodus and the Covenant, Sinai and God—what are Ahab and Jezebel and the vicious threats of a proud heart beside the things that God has set His hand to, and the things that once for all time took place?

Even so to the Christian heart. His baptism, his Damascus Road, his Emmaus, and many a private Horeb, point the way out of dejected moods to stable and unfaltering faith. Even more does the service of the Lord's Table become to despondent, sore-pressed hearts a Christian Horeb, where we stand on another Hill, remembering another Covenant, and a Greater Moses. How truly the Saviour understood these vacillating hearts of ours, and knew the need of fixed, unalterable things to impart to our inconstant nature permanence, patience, and persistence. "This do in remembrance of Me" . . . Come away out of yourself, your moods, your feelings of despair; fix your gaze on that which God hath wrought. "Remember . . ."—this is the *place* for the downcast to pray, on the standing-ground of fact, and history, and God's unchangeable deed. Happy the man who when strength fails or plans miscarry has a Horeb to which to flee. Even Jesus, when first the Galileans turned away, and again as He set out for Calvary, found solace in a mountain-top of prayer.

III

And what happened to Elijah there? The great thing which prayer did for the prophet's own heart was to bring him to a far truer judgement concerning the ways of God. He learned, for example, something unforgettable concerning God *methods*.

For long, with eager eyes, Elijah had looked for the signs that God was working in the life of Israel; for a wind of God that should sweep irresistibly away the new evils and the older errors that beset the nation's soul; for a searching, scorching fire of judgement that should consume at one blast the immoral idolatries that his soul hated; for a spiritual earthquake that should undermine and overthrow, dramatically and finally, the throne of Ahab and all the ascendant forces of heathenism that held God's people in thrall. He wanted, and had waited for that kind of divine intervention—even as John the Baptist, coming "in the spirit and power of Elias" long afterwards, waited for the Messiah with an axe, and fan and fire of judgement. Both in their time looked for a divine intervention that should be sudden, overwhelming, irresistible, consuming, and final. "But God was not in the wind . . . not in the earthquake . . . not in the fire."

God would have His servant learn that in the still small voice of the awakening conscience of the nation there was far greater promise of ultimate reform than in any forcible revolution; that God in fact very often does speak to a generation in "a sound of gentle stillness". Elijah discovered it is wrong to assume that whenever God is at work there must be blood and fire and noise and power. Elijah, like John the Baptist, must adjust his thinking to the truth that God works in quiet, gracious ways, by unseen processes, and the mills of God grind often silently.

> Thrice blest is he to whom is given
> The instinct that can tell
> That God is on the field, when He
> Is most invisible.

Elijah learned something equally unforgettable about God's *resources*. On the height of Horeb he gained a new perspective from which his despairing viewpoint seemed childishly narrow and self-centred. He had said the work was hopeless, the cause was lost, and he was ready to die—because he alone remained faithful and his life was in danger! Here is zealous concern, and self-importance, and despondency strangely— but not at all unusually—mixed. It seemed to Elijah that what was happening to himself was the crux of the whole situation facing God in Israel! We are all prone to judge the whole course of the war from what is happening on our bit of the front. But no, says God—"seven thousand in Israel" beside you, Elijah—"seven thousand, all the knees which have not bowed unto Baal, and every mouth which hath not kissed him". These already God has marked as faithful, and will spare. How different the spiritual battlefield looks when you get high enough on Horeb to see it from God's perspective;

and how much less important your own feelings and failures become.

And Elijah learned, once more, in his time of communion with God on Horeb, the further unforgettable lesson of God's unhurried but undeviating *purpose*. While Elijah despairs about the future, God is planning for it. God had His scourge ready to chasten Israel, in the new king of Damascus, whom Elijah was to go forthwith and anoint. God had ready a new king for Israel, to supplant Ahab, the strong, Cromwellian Jehu—and to his immediate anointing also the prophet is sent. More wonderful still, while Elijah is bemoaning his solitary faithfulness to God, God has ready a successor in the prophetic office—Elisha, and to him again Elijah is sent.

This is God's unanswerable reply to Elijah's despondency about the future—to go and set on foot a movement which would accomplish things beyond anything Elijah could imagine. The men of God may get downcast, the battle go ill, the signs of the times be unpropitious, the boldest warriors turn and flee, but God's eternal thought moves on His undisturbed affairs. His purpose halts not, nor hesitates, is never caught unready, nor outwitted by evil. Always God has His men and His movement prepared, His instrument fashioned, His next move already afoot. For His purpose is unswerving, and invincible.

IV

Such is Elijah's place in the Old Testament's varied exploration of the meanings of prayer. To Israel and to Ahab, (and to James) his praying spoke of power, and of judgement upon Israel. In the depths of his own heart's experience, when God humbled and uplifted him, he knew the prayer that brings a truer judgement about God's methods, resources, and unchanging purpose. Horeb brought new understanding, that sent him back to the task, chastened no doubt, but with the faith and hope that brought him in the end to glory, riding in chariots of fire.

None of us needs to be told that spiritual discouragement is an uncomfortable, *miserable* experience. It is not so often realised that it is also extremely dangerous. It paralyses the will, clouds the faith, silences the testimony. It often loses us great opportunities, defeats and disarms us in the hour of conflict, burdens us with complaints, plunges us into self-pity. and keeps us idle when there is work to be done. All too often discouragement makes us careless, neglectful, even wilful; the despondent heart so very easily becomes a rebellious heart. And very, very often discouragement silences prayer.

Yet prayer is discouragement's only real cure. Other things may soothe and comfort us, but it takes prayer like Elijah's to set us on our feet again. We look, when our hearts are downcast, for some change in circumstances, a turning of the tide; we seek the spiritual "tonic" of great meetings or beloved messengers; we work and pray for personal success. But courage so kindled will still remain dependent upon the flow of current events, the happenings we cannot control. We shall soon be despondent again. The lasting cure of all discouragement is to seek out Our Lord and let Him talk to us of the right assessment of things.

As the discouraged disciples sat in Galilee listening to the illuminating parable about the varied results of faithful sowing, and the explanation Jesus gave why so many turned away; as the heart-broken two walked with Him to Emmaus and felt their hearts burn within them as He explained to them the Scripture's forecast of Messiah's suffering—so with Elijah we may retire to some Horeb and let the Master bring us again to a right judgement about His work and ourselves.

Prayer brings the better understanding in which a clear-eyed courage finds its strength; that is Elijah's word to pessimistic Christians and disheartened workers for God. Pray—you'll understand better, and not faint.

JEHOSHAPHAT: THE KEYNOTE OF PRAYER

"*And Jehoshaphat the king of Judah returned to his house in peace to Jerusalem. And Jehu the son of Hanani the seer went out to meet him, and said to king Jehoshaphat, Shouldest thou help the wicked, and love them that hate the Lord? for this thing wrath is upon thee from the Lord. Nevertheless there are good things found in thee . . . And Jehoshaphat set himself to seek unto the Lord . . . And Jehoshaphat stood in the congregation of Judah and Jerusalem, in the house of the Lord . . . and he said, O Lord, the God of our fathers, art not thou God in heaven? and art not thou ruler over all the kingdoms of the nations? and in thine hand is power and might, so that none is able to withstand thee . . . And now, behold the children of Ammon and Moab and Mount Seir, whom thou wouldest not let Israel invade, when they came out of the land of Egypt . . . behold how they reward us, to come to cast us out of thy possession . . . O our God, wilt thou not judge them? for we have no might against this great company that cometh against us; neither know we what to do: but our eyes are upon thee . . . Then upon Jahaziel . . . came the spirit of the Lord in the midst of the congregation; and he said, Hearken ye, all Judah, and ye inhabitants of Jerusalem, and thou king Jehoshaphat: Thus saith the Lord unto you, Fear not ye, neither be dismayed by reason of this great multitude; for the battle is not yours, but God's.*"

2 CHRONICLES 19: 1–3; 20: 3–15

THE PARTICULAR CONTRIBUTION WHICH KING JEHOSHA-
phat has to make to our studies of prayer and its
implications is closely related to the lesson which was
taught us by Asa, his father. Asa reminded us that true prayer
proceeds upon the assumption that in all circumstances, even
against overwhelming odds and in seemingly inescapable
predicaments, reliance may be placed unhesitatingly and
fearlessly upon God who heareth prayer. In short, prayer *is*
reliance upon God expressed in supplication. King Jehoshaphat has one especial addition to make to that statement,
but the point is so clearly illustrated by his life that we do
well to begin not with the words of his prayer and the answer
he received, but with his story.

I

Jehoshaphat began to reign at the age of thirty-five, which
implies that his most formative years of training were those
of Asa's earlier and better period. He followed what the
Chronicler hinted were the "first ways" of his father. One
thing emphasised about Jehoshaphat is his strength—his
might, and his warring. He built and fortified numerous cities,
he created and armed an enormous force, reputedly over a
million men. His policy might be described as that of friendship through strength, and he sought and maintained for most
of his reign a successful peace, of a somewhat ambiguous
kind, with most of his neighbours. The quality of that peace
depends upon whether we view the "presents" of the Philistines
and Arabs as gifts, tribute, or bribes. There is little doubt
that Israel too, the divided kingdom of the north, felt that in
Jehoshaphat she had to deal with one whose strength demanded
respect. She plainly concluded that alliance was more profitable
than hostility.

Similar emphasis is laid upon Jehoshaphat's great wealth

and expanding trade. Great store cities and palaces are described, and the comfortable materialistic outlook of the time is expressed in the eulogy "God gave him wealth and honour" —wealth being, to the author, a proof of divine blessing. It is a little surprising to learn of Jehoshaphat's attempt to emulate Solomon the Magnificent in sending gold-ships to Ophir, a round trip of three years. Though the venture was unsuccessful, the Jewish historians record the attempt with considerable pride, as testimony to Jehoshaphat's greatness.

Nor was the king's religious zeal lacking in intensity or initiative. He courageously set on foot certain moral reforms connected with the prevalent religious prostitution, and supervised arrangements for the better education of his people by the help of Princes, Levites, and a book of the Law. Remembering the religious preoccupations of the writers of Chronicles we are the more impressed with the repeated tributes paid to all these excellencies in the character of Jehoshaphat: "So the realm of Jehoshaphat was quiet, for his God gave him rest round about . . . Therefore the Lord stablished the kingdom in his hand; and all Judah brought to Jehoshaphat presents; and he had riches and honour in abundance. And his heart was lifted up in the ways of the Lord: and furthermore he took away the high places and the Asherim out of Judah" (the latter referring to the places and the symbols associated with unclean pagan rites). Altogether, the picture given us is of a strong, wealthy, successful and religious King of Judah.

II

What then could endanger one whose heart was lifted up in the ways of the Lord, and whose wealth and kingdom the Lord had established? The Chronicler himself supplies the answer with sharpened brevity: "Now Jehoshaphat had riches and honour in abundance; and he joined affinity with Ahab".

There lay the weak spot in Jehoshaphat's armour, the cunning trap set for his unwary feet. Ahab is Israel's wickedest king to date, husband of the notorious Jezebel, enemy of Elijah. What has Jehoshaphat to do with such a man? Even the Chronicler implies the spiritual folly and certain loss involved in such alliance with the worldling in his sin, and helps us see the gradual declension by which the good king was brought low.

First comes a marriage compact—apparently between Ahab's daughter and Jehoshaphat's son Jehoram. This undoubtedly had implications both of political alliance and social equality. It led inevitably to the second step, a formal and luxurious and prolonged Eastern visit, a meeting of the heads of States, each determined not to be outdone in magnificence and generosity, yet each watchful of the other's secret motives. Then finally there grows a pact for joint military operations.

It is fairly plain that Jehoshaphat was led farther by the wily Ahab than he had intended to go. Ramoth in Gilead was now in Syrian hands, but had been Israel's in the days before the Israelite disruption. It was therefore a long-standing grievance which southern as well as northern hearts would share; and one Jehoshaphat was morally bound to help remove—though not with such as Ahab for his ally.

Jehoshaphat's conscience was doubtless uneasy; and his shrewd caution bade him go carefully. He was not by any means wholehearted in his friendship for Ahab for he had diligently fortified his frontier against Ahab's designs. The visit was very much a clasping of mailed fists! Jehoshaphat too had refused Ahab's offered help in the matter of the gold-ships—he knew his Ahab! And the statement "Jehoshaphat did not after the doings of Israel" seems to preserve an echo of southern contempt towards some of the things Jehoshaphat witnessed at the court of the northern kingdom. In view of all this, it was surely with his tongue in his cheek that Jehoshaphat replied to Ahab's suggestion about attacking Ramoth

Gilead, "I am as thou art, and my people as thy people; and we will be with thee in the war."

As with all unconsecrated alliances, the commitment grew beyond intention but conscience continued its protests. *After* he has made his promise, Jehoshaphat urges Ahab to enquire of the word of the Lord. Ahab—knowing his Jehoshaphat as well as Jehoshaphat knew him!—puts on a religious demonstration calculated to impress anyone not already secretly convicted of wrong: four hundred of Ahab's prophets unite to pronounce divine approval of the scheme.

Yet the king of Judah's unquiet conscience will not be easy, for he knows that Ahab's hireling prophets are only for propaganda purposes. Asking for another, independent voice, he is given Micaiah, son of Imlah, worthy successor to Nathan, and fore-runner of Jeremiah, John the Baptist, Peter before the Sanhedrin, and all the rest of the long line of heroes of the unconsenting conscience confronting Authority with the truth. Micaiah boldly tells Ahab that the expedition will end in disaster. But an uneasy conscience, even when fortified by so clear a word from God, may still be too weak, too involved already in unholy compromise, to resolve aright. Jehoshaphat supinely acquiesces in the imprisonment of the man whose testimony he had sought, and goes forth to fight beside Ahab.

The children of this world are wiser in their generation than the children of light. Sly Ahab persuades Jehoshaphat to enter battle royally clad while he himself fights incognito. Thus the fiercest fighting is decoyed around Judah's king— who (as is ever the case when God's men join hands with the ungodly) is himself mistaken for the worldling. God in mercy shelters the weak and foolish king; Ahab is slain, the battle lost, and Jehoshaphat is glad to escape from the entanglement with his life.

Returning home to Judah, his proud strength humbled, his policy disgraced, he is met by another faithful man of God, with the searching question: "Shouldest thou help the wicked, and love them that hate the Lord?" The experience, and the rebuke, struck home, and Jehoshaphat turns with chastened spirit to his real work in Judah. He "went out again among the people from Beersheba to the hill country of Ephraim, and brought them back unto the Lord, the God of their fathers. And he set judges in the land ... and said to the judges, Consider what ye do: for ye judge not for man, but for the Lord; and he is with you in giving judgement. Now therefore let the fear of the Lord be upon you; take heed and do it: for there is no iniquity with the Lord our God, nor respect of persons, nor taking of gifts." And he set Levites, priests and heads of families for magistrates, under the same religious responsibility, urging them to "Deal courageously, and the Lord be with the good". Of the value of such reforms in the ancient East it is unnecessary to speak. Jehoshaphat is again a diligent and godly king; the backslider has returned.

But repentance cannot always avert the consequences of the wrong we do. The results of Jehoshaphat's misbegotten alliance with Ahab must yet be faced. How far his army was mauled at Ramoth we are not told, but certainly the defeat before Syria reduced his prestige among surrounding nations— and prestige was three parts of power in that political world. Little nations like Ammon, Moab, and Arab marauders from the districts about Mount Seir see their opportunity for plunder and revenge, and conspiring together threaten Judah's unfortified eastern flank.

No million men, no strong cities, no foreign alliances support Jehoshaphat now. "Jehoshaphat feared, and set himself to seek the Lord; and he proclaimed a fast throughout all Judah. And Judah gathered themselves together to seek help of the Lord". "And Jehoshaphat stood in the congregation of Judah and Jerusalem in the house of the Lord" and he prayed.

III

Jehoshaphat's prayer gains immeasurably in significance in the light of the story that lay behind it. He begins with thought of the divine sovereignty over all nations. He recalls the original purpose that Israel should possess this land, and the promises of divine protection renewed at the building of the Temple. He remembers too that God forbade the invasion of the neighbouring peoples who now endanger Judah, and pleads "O our God, wilt thou not judge them? for we have no might against this great company that cometh against us; neither know we what to do; but our eyes are upon thee." "We have no might . . . our eyes are upon thee"; this is the keynote of Jehoshaphat's plea. And what lends it forcefulness is the memory that not so long before his eyes were on Ahab and his might—he supposed—lay in a strong army and a foreign alliance. The keynote of Jehoshaphat's prayer is reliance upon God—*alone*.

That is also the theme of the unexpected reply immediately vouchsafed to the King through the coming of the Spirit upon Jahaziel: "Fear not ye, neither be dismayed by reason of this great multitude; for the battle is not yours, but God's. . . . Ye shall not need to fight in this battle: set yourselves, stand ye still, and see the salvation of the Lord with you, O Judah and Jerusalem: fear not, nor be dismayed: tomorrow go out against them; for the Lord is with you." The words echo very closely (and perhaps deliberately) the words of Moses to Israel at the brink of the Red Sea, with the Egyptians in hot pursuit. For the situation is much the same—God's people need to learn again, as they learned then, that the power to save lies in God *alone*.

Jehoshaphat's response is to bow in worship. Then he set the army in array overlooking the battlefield, addressing them the next morning with the brave words "Hear me, O Judah, and ye inhabitants of Jerusalem; believe in the Lord your God, so shall ye be established; believe His prophets, so shall ye prosper." The appointed singers led a song of thanksgiving—before the "battle" had begun!—and all Judah watched as the words of Jahaziel were literally fulfilled before their eyes.

Then Jehoshaphat was read a new and sharp lesson on the peril of ill-conceived alliances. The rough-and-ready conspiracy of Moab, Ammon, and the Arabs fell asunder, and those so unequally yoked together proceeded to slay each other. Israel had only to gather up the rich spoils, which took three days; to rename the valley "The Valley of Blessing"; and to return in gladness and thanksgiving to Jerusalem.

IV

The strategy of spiritual conflict varies with the circumstances. Occasionally, the right thing to do is to evade a head-on clash with forces too strong for us, by a wise readjustment of the situation—"It came to pass, when Pharaoh had let the people go, that God led them not by the way of the land of the Philistines, although that was near; for God said, Lest peradventure the people repent when they see war, and they return to Egypt: but God led the people about, by the way of the wilderness by the Red Sea." If the end be gained without loss of principle, it is better that conflict be avoided.

Sometimes, as with Paul's advice to Timothy to "Flee youthful lusts", the right strategy for conflict is flight. To make no provisions for the flesh, is to forestall temptation, thus insuring against defeat by admitting beforehand that you are likely to fall, and cutting out of life all that gives occasion to the enemy.

Sometimes, of course, it is necessary to fight, clothed with all available armour, with the Lord's standard raised high over the hillside, as when Israel fought Amalek, and with resolution, endurance and sacrifice to maintain the Lord's cause. The heroic, military element cannot be wholly excluded from Christian discipleship.

But then there are times when the right strategy is to stand still and see the Lord's victory. Jehoshaphat must learn that on occasion his might and his warring, his army and his prowess, his alliances and his resolution are all irrelevant, for the Lord will fight for him, and the battle is God's. Perhaps this is specially true when injustice has been done against ourselves, or when our pride has been hurt, our work criticised, our motives impugned. Then it is best, and right, to "commit ourselves to Him that judgeth righteously" and who will maintain our cause, and "be with the good". It needs self-discipline, and deep faith, to "*stand still* and see the salvation of God". But it can issue in amazed and humbled thanksgiving.

Is it not true that we sometimes do dishonour to the cause we defend and to the Master we serve, by the weapons we are ready to use, the alliances we are willing to enter, to gain our ends? "If the wrong man uses the right means, the right means work in the wrong way" is a shrewd saying of Lao Tse. Sometimes the right man using the wrong means, or calling to his aid the wrong allies, finds the same result. The man of prayer learns with Asa to place reliance upon God, and with Asa's son that oftentimes this means upon God *alone*. Weapons unworthy of the cause can injure the hands that wield them, and allies who are not of God's choosing subtract from our real strength. For the battle is not ours, but God's.

v

Upon God alone! No one has ever loved men, and human companionship more than Jesus did. Nor has anyone laid such emphasis upon the need for fellowship in the work of God, for oneness of mind, and love of each other, and the unity that shall impress the world. Yet in the crucial hours, though He chose that others should be near at hand, He is still the lonely Christ. When multitudes throng His days, He will rise up a great while before day and seek a lonely place to pray. Before choosing the Twelve, He spends a night alone upon the mountain. When the crowd He had fed seeks in unthinking excitement to make Him king, He disappears alone to pray, and on the Mount of Transfiguration and in the garden of Gethsemane the disciples sleep and leave Him alone with God.

Not less, but infinitely more than we, Jesus knew the inner citadel of prayer where great decisions must be taken, battles fought, serenity renewed, guidance received, when the heart has turned from others to seek God—alone. Peter's sword is His to command, and legions of angels await His beckoning. But neither these, nor yet men, to whom He would not trust Himself, knowing what was in them, are used in His support. He will trust in God alone, with a sublime concentration of faith upon One who is sufficient in Himself and needs no help.

Jehoshaphat's lesson must not be erected into a universal principle of Christian isolationism. There are times when the word that will come to us is to seek the counsel and support of godly friends, and feed upon the means of grace provided by the fellowship of saints. But occasionally the situation facing us resembles that of Jehoshaphat with Ahab, and then the necessary warning is "Shouldest thou help the wicked, and love them that hate the Lord?" Then the prayerful heart will turn from all weakening, unworthy, ill-conceived alliances *to trust in the Lord alone, for in Him is all sufficiency, and there is none beside Him.*

HEZEKIAH: THE LIFE-LINE OF PRAYER

"*Then came the word of the Lord to Isaiah, saying, Go, and say to Hezekiah, Thus saith the Lord, the God of David, thy father, I have heard thy prayer, I have seen thy tears: behold, I will add unto thy days fifteen years. And I will deliver thee and this city out of the hand of the king of Assyria: and I will defend this city . . . The writing of Hezekiah king of Judah, when he had been sick, and was recovered of his sickness. I said, In the noontide of my days I shall go into the gates of the grave: I am deprived of the residue of my years. I said, I shall not see the Lord, even the Lord in the land of the living: I shall behold man no more with the inhabitants of the world. Mine age is removed, and is carried away from me as a shepherd's tent: I have rolled up like a weaver my life; he will cut me off from the loom. . . . Like a swallow or a crane, so did I chatter: I did mourn as a dove: mine eyes fail with looking upward; O Lord I am oppressed, be thou my surety. What shall I say? He hath both spoken unto me, and himself hath done it: I shall go softly all my years because of the bitterness of my soul. O Lord, by these things men live, and wholly therein is the life of my spirit: wherefore recover thou me, and make me to live. Behold, it was for my peace that I had great bitterness: but thou hast in love to my soul delivered it from the pit of corruption; for thou hast cast all my sins behind thy back. For the grave cannot praise thee, death cannot celebrate thee: they that go down into the pit cannot hope for thy truth. The living, the living, he shall praise thee, as I do this day. . . .*"

ISAIAH 38: 4–20

IT IS SIGNIFICANT, AND RIGHT, THAT ONLY TOWARDS THE END of this series of lessons on prayer do we reach the one point about prayer which many people would place first—that prayer is the religious man's way out of trouble, a means of flight from adversity. We saw in Jabez' example that prayer is the way of escape from evil in heredity and environment. In Hezekiah it is rather the escape from trouble of more literal and material kinds.

Superficial minds, unpractised in the life of prayer, often assume that this is all that prayer means, a life-line thrown out in an emergency. They dismiss prayer scornfully, in consequence, as the escape-mechanism of weak and cowardly spirits for whom reality is too hard; or else as sheer hypocrisy, calling upon God when fears assail but careless of Him when all goes well. It is worth while to emphasise therefore that the Bible has read us eleven lessons on prayer before speaking of this.

We have seen prayer as intercession, as spiritual equipment for great tasks, as the guardian of conscience; as the secret of daring, of faithfulness, and of forgiveness; as the expression of national piety; as deliverance from evil; and as the source of spiritual insight, true judgements and deep confidence. All this before we come upon an example of one to whom prayer seems at first sight to be mainly a way of getting what he wants, especially as a way out of adversity. We must not by any means despise this value and function of prayer-experience, but it is wise to observe the Scriptural proportion and emphasis in this respect. Prayer is more, very, very much more, than asking for *things*. Nevertheless, Jesus bade us ask for bread.

I

Hezekiah is one of Scripture's favourites, and his story is a full and notable one, most of it twice-told. But the facts we need to notice are soon recounted. He was a faithful, godly king of Judah, who set his authority and great courage firmly against superstition and idolatry, even (in the case of the brazen serpent which Moses had made and which, now an idol, was destroyed at the king's command) in the face of popular antagonism and misrepresentation of his motives. But he saw, perhaps, more than his share of trouble, and in trouble learned his insights into the power of prayer.

Before, during and after Hezekiah's reign the whole of Palestine was under the imperial government of Assyria. For most of Hezekiah's time, the tiny Palestinian states seethed with resentment and revolt—a situation which Egypt did her best to fan into open rebellion. Foolishly, Hezekiah joined in the general restlessness by withholding tribute from Assyria, and called down upon Judah the threat of invasion and destruction. A grim object-lesson on the meaning of such a threat lay before his eyes in the ruin of the northern kingdom, Israel. Then Hezekiah sent off lavish gifts, but too little, and too late, to satisfy the emperor Sennacherib, who despatched a force to besiege the city and a cunning orator to woo the people's loyalty.

Hezekiah's reaction was to beseech the prophet Isaiah to pray for the city, urging that God avenge the blasphemy of the eloquent Rabshakeh. Isaiah promised that rumours of trouble elsewhere would lead to the withdrawal of the forces before Jerusalem and the total deliverance of the city—and so it happened. Hezekiah has had his first lesson on the practical power of prayer.

A year or two later Abyssinia revolted from Assyrian rule, and Sennacherib's forces again came westwards. To secure his long and thinly guarded supply-lines, the commander, while making for the Egyptian border, sent a token contingent to threaten Jerusalem with dire vengeance if she dared take action on his flank. Hezekiah took the threat seriously, and receiving the letter from the embassy brought it into the Temple to spread it out before the Lord.

This time his prayer begins with the supremacy of God over all nations of the earth, and pleads that God will take note of the words of Sennacherib: "Incline thine ear, O Lord, and hear; open thine eyes, O Lord, and see: and hear all the words of Sennacherib, which hath sent to reproach the living God. Of a truth, Lord, the kings of Assyria have laid waste all the countries, and their land, and have cast their gods into the fire: for they were no gods, but the work of men's hands, wood and stone; therefore they have destroyed them. Now therefore, O Lord our God, save us from his hand, that all the kingdoms of the earth may know that thou art the Lord, even thou only."

Again the answer came through Isaiah the prophet, but this time in the form of a powerful and exulting taunt-song for "the virgin daughter of Israel" to sing in the face of the enemy. The song recounts at length the proud boasts of the Assyrians but says that God is well aware of every Assyrian secret, and will end her arrogance. Her mighty force now on Egypt's frontier shall become a mere fish on the angler's hook, a horse close-bridled by a powerful hand, and at God's word shall be drawn back "to the place whence it came". The song goes on to predict that Judah shall have peace and prosperity, neither arrow nor shield nor earthwork shall approach Jerusalem, "For I will defend this city to save it, for mine own sake, and for my servant David's sake".

And thus it was. In the armed camp of Assyria the angel of death visited in a single night 185,000 of the imperial army, "so Sennacherib king of Assyria departed, and went and returned, and dwelt at Nineveh."

Assyrian records merely show an abrupt return to Nineveh, without meeting Abyssinia or visiting Jerusalem, and in the twenty years that remained of Sennacherib's reign never another Syrian campaign. Herodotus however preserves an Egyptian story of field-mice that ate the bow-strings, bridles and shield straps of Assyria's force, and tells of a statue of the Egyptian king in the Temple of Hephaestus having a mouse upon his hand. It is also reported that a Persian army met destruction by disease at this very frontier four centuries before Christ. From this same source spread a devastating plague in the time of Justinian, and here also the Crusades met virulent infection. The connection of rats, bubonic plague, the Serbonian bog and Isaiah's Angel of Death is not hard to see —and another Bible miracle in answer to prayer is incontestably confirmed.

Hezekiah's third experience of trouble is of a more private nature. A sharp and perilous sickness befell him, and the warning of the prophet was that he must prepare for death. Once more the king turned in extremity to prayer, appealing this time with flowing tears to the divine pity, and pleading his sincerity in all God's ways—"Remember now, O Lord, I beseech thee, how I have walked before thee in truth and with a perfect heart (that is, whole-heartedly) and have done that which is good in thy sight".

God's answer came in gracious and memorable words: "Thus saith the Lord, the God of David thy father, I have heard thy prayer, I have seen thy tears: behold, I will add unto thy days fifteen years." And a moving Psalm of thanksgiving was the king's response to a third experience of prayer's potency in the day of adversity.

II

Neither brilliant nor wise, nor yet a pioneer in spiritual things, Hezekiah was nevertheless a good king, faithful and humble, and sincere of purpose. His reign was uneasy, his task unwelcome, his experience overfull of trouble, but he did discover in his weakness and lack of wisdom a life-line to keep his head above the threatening waters. He worked out in practical experience a worthwhile lesson on the prayer that finds God a very present help in life's emergencies.

He has some simple commonsense to offer, for example,

about the *precautions* of such prayer: the close relation, in this realm of prayer-experience, of supplication and self-help. While he prays, he sends off the stupidly withheld tribute, with lavish extra gifts; he attempts an answer to the Assyrian orator's arguments; he willingly accepts the medical ministration of Isaiah, and his "plaister of figs". The simple point is not always remembered by those who speak much of "material" answers to prayer.

Of course God—whose are all things—will hear our prayer about material needs: about our daily bread, our food, raiment, shelter, health, work and every other human concern. But *we* must do our share. The answer to "Give us this day our daily bread" may well be "In the sweat of thy brow shalt thou eat bread". . . . "If any man will not work, neither shall he eat." James urges that we pray together for the sick, but he advises also the use of oil—the obvious and universal palliative of the East, a sort of first-century aspirin.

Some think too that this is the real point of Christ's reply to Peter about the payment of the tribute-money. The advice to go down to the water's edge and take up the first fish, which shall have a coin in its mouth, may be a way of telling Peter— "Why ask me for it, Peter: you are a fisherman, you have a boat and net, and there is the sea!" The interpretation is highly uncertain, but not impossible, for certainly Jesus held no brief for pious laziness. Prayer is not magic : the man of God in trouble will turn to faith—and figs!

It is instructive too in this connection to notice Hezekiah's *pleas*. Though he asks material help, he does not seek to use the throne of mercy as a bargain counter. He knows that health and the prolongation of life cannot be divorced from spiritual integrity and piety. When he appeals for pity for himself, he pleads his own sincere attempts to walk in God's ways, and his own deep sorrow. When the need is wider, it is of God's name and honour that he thinks, and of the reproach and blasphemy of Assyria's spokesmen.

He might have pleaded his own fears, and the desperate need of the city, the longing for relief, escape, deliverance— and who should blame him? But such prayer would have been less memorable, perhaps less prevailing. Even though the petition be for material and emergency help, the basis of our asking is still concern for the divine purpose and will. Even our Gethsemanes proceed on this assumption. We may ask for some bitter cup to pass, but it is "Nevertheless not my will, but Thine" which qualifies our petition, as it did our Master's.

Nor should we miss the marked *progress* which Hezekiah shows in this discipline of "life-line" prayer. John Owen speaks of the way in which men are sometimes driven to pray by sudden shocks of pain. When faced with difficulties, there is a voice in human nature that cries out immediately to the God of nature, so that men on such occasions are surprised into calling on the name of God. But the purely instinctive reaction, found to be successful, may become an exercise; the exercise a habit, and the habit an art of prayerful living. Something like this is reflected in the simple facts that Hezekiah at first sends to Isaiah, asking the prophet to pray for him; next he prays in the Temple, spreading Sennacherib's letter before the Lord; and next he prays in the privacy of his own chamber with tears and broken words.

But still more plainly is the king's spiritual progress seen in the beautiful Psalm of his thanksgiving. The experience of sickness left its mark. He says that henceforth he will go in solemn procession, for life has now a new dignity, a deeper value, an increased sacredness. As life was slipping away he came to see what *made* life, and his Psalm recounts the harvest of new insights he has gathered from the fields of sickness, what he calls "the things by which men live".

First is the realisation that "God hath spoken unto me, and Himself hath performed it". A divine visitation, a wholly new and nearer experience of the hand of God upon his life, the voice of God within his soul—this Hezekiah has found through his urgent, heartfelt cry for aid. Finding this, he feels he has begun to live.

Second, "Thou hast in love to my soul delivered it from the pit of corruption, for Thou hast cast all my sins behind Thy back". Sickness and the approach of death have sharpened his conscience, fear and weakness have searched his soul, but with the new knowledge of God's visiting him has come the new knowledge of God's forgiving him. By these things, says the good king with opened eyes, men *live*—by the divine touch on their lives and the divine pardon in their hearts. Small wonder that he could affirm "It was for my peace that I had great bitterness" and add "The living, the living, he shall praise Thee, as I do this day".

This is the great blessing and beauty of "the lower levels of prayer"—*the petitions for material and urgent need, though sometimes they seem insincere and worldly, selfish and circumscribed, childish and superficial, nevertheless are met with the everlasting mercy. And the man who in these things has found God faithful will not be content with these alone, but will seek God in the fullness of His gifts and grace.* The life-line may become a ladder, the emergency an exploration, the first simple "God help me!" begin a lifetime of prayer-discovery.

HABAKKUK: THE MATURITY OF PRAYER

"*O Lord, how long shall I cry, and thou wilt not hear? I cry out unto thee of violence, and thou wilt not save. . . . I will stand upon my watch, and set me upon the tower, and will look forth to see what he will speak with me, and what I shall answer concerning my complaint. And the Lord answered me, and said, Write the vision and make it plain upon tables, that he may run that readeth it. For the vision is yet for the appointed time, and it hasteth toward the end, and shall not lie: though it tarry, wait for it; because it will surely come, it will not delay. Behold his soul is puffed up, it is not upright in him: but the just shall live by his faith. . . . For though the figtree shall not blossom, neither shall fruit be in the vines; the labour of the olive shall fail, and the fields shall yield no meat; the flock shall be cut off from the fold, and there shall be no herd in the stalls: yet I will rejoice in the Lord, I will joy in the God of my salvation. Jehovah, the Lord, is my strength, and he maketh my feet like hinds' feet, and will make me to walk upon mine high places.*"

HABAKKUK 1: 2; 2: 1–4; 3: 17–19

AFTER HEZEKIAH—HABAKKUK. AFTER THE PRAYER WHICH cries to God to get the things it needs, the prayer which clings to God and confidently goes without. After the life-line thrown out for rescue from adversity, the mature faith that accepts adversity—and deep perplexity—in the conviction that having God it has all things. There is abundant room in the Christian life for both kinds of faith, and both levels of prayer. The Christian follows One who had not where to lay His head, yet he knows with Paul that all things are his as he is Christ's and Christ is God's. Like the Apostle, the experienced Christian has been initiated into the secret, in whatsoever state he is therein to be content. He knows how to go hungry and how to have abundance, he can undergo all things in Christ who strengthens him. Sometimes he will kneel with Hezekiah to ask that God will give, but at other times he will give thanks with Habakkuk to the God who has withheld all things—except Himself. And this in spite of serious perplexity of mind.

I

Apart from the meagre facts that he was a Hebrew "prophet" living about 600 years before Christ, the author of two chapters of the Scripture and (a little less certainly) of an exquisite poem which constitutes a third chapter, we know nothing whatever of Habakkuk, of his parents, home, children or occupation, nor even whether he ministered in any public way at all. Nothing is clear about him except the question he asked, the answer he received, and the high level of spiritual insight and mature faith which they enshrine.

Like other prophets, Habakkuk was concerned about the evil that for so long goes unpunished. He was deeply perplexed by the way that the wicked seem allowed to oppress the righteous, and wrong to triumph over right. "O Lord, how long shall I cry and thou wilt not hear? I cry out unto thee of violence, and thou wilt not save. Why dost thou show me iniquity, and look upon perverseness? for spoiling and violence are before me: and there is strife, and contention riseth up. Therefore the law is slacked, and judgement doth never go forth: for the wicked doth compass about the righteous; therefore judgement goeth forth perverted".

And the prophet received an answer. On the horizon stands an instrument of divine punishment, which shall bring wrath upon the evil leaders of too complacent Israel—the dreaded Chaldean army. "Behold ye among the nations, and regard, and wonder marvellously: for I work a work in your days, which ye will not believe though it be told you. For lo, I raise up the Chaldeans, that bitter and hasty nation; which march through the breadth of the earth, to possess dwelling places that are not theirs. They are terrible and dreadful. . . . Their horses also are swifter than leopards, and are more fierce than the evening wolves; and their horsemen spread themselves: yea, their horsemen come from afar; they fly as an eagle that hasteth to devour. They come all of them for violence; their faces are set eagerly as the east wind; and they gather captives as the sand. Yea he scoffeth at kings, and princes are a derision unto him; he derideth every stronghold, for he heapeth up dust (earthen ramparts) and taketh it. Then they sweep by like the wind and go on, guilty men, whose own might is their god!"

This is an answer sufficient for the problem which faces the prophet within Israel. The wicked shall surely, and swiftly, reap the ill reward of their ways, and evil shall not go unrequited. But Habakkuk's vision is not confined to Israel: the Lord is God of the whole earth, and Chaldea's wickedness matters to God no less than Israel's. So the problem arises on a larger canvas. How can God use the Chaldeans to chastise Israel? why shall the more wicked correct the less wicked? why should violence, injustice, cruelty, avarice, triumph even in Chaldea?

"O Lord thou hast ordained him for judgement; and thou O Rock, hast established him for correction. Thou that art of purer eyes than to behold evil, and that canst not look on perverseness, wherefore lookest thou upon them that deal treacherously, and holdest thy peace when the wicked swalloweth the man that is more righteous than he; and makest men as the fishes of the sea, as the creeping things that have no ruler over them? He taketh up all of them with the angle, he catcheth them in his net, and gathereth them in his drag:

therefore he rejoiceth and is glad. Therefore he sacrificeth unto his net, and burneth incense unto his drag; because by them his portion is fat, and his meat plenteous. Shall he therefore empty his net (continually) and not spare to slay the nations continually?"

It is the age-old, searching problem of the moral government of the world. It is striking that it should be asked twenty-six centuries ago—but the Hebrew prophets were profound and forthright thinkers. It is significant, too, that the question arises in Judaism, for it is only where the goodness and justice of God are clearly affirmed that the problem of evil and its power is felt as a perplexity of faith. Where the gods themselves are thought to be capricious and amoral, the existence of evil explains itself. Against the background of the Hebrew vision of God, experience of the world and its moral tragedies clamours for explanation. How shall a man keep his faith in God in an evil time, when wrong triumphs and the innocent suffer and the wicked swalloweth up the man that is more righteous than he? Habakkuk takes the heart-shaking question in prayer to God.

II

Here is one mark of Habakkuk's maturity of faith. God's ways are a mystery, His methods seem unjust and wrong. But just where many cease to pray, by reason of perplexity of faith, *because* they cannot understand, Habakkuk brings his prayer—*because* he cannot understand. He seeks explanation where alone explanation might be found. He pleads not for gifts or goodness but for light to live by, for understanding to succour a doubting soul, for grace to comprehend God's ways. There is a boldness about his questioning, a daring in his conversation with God about the way God does things: and a refreshing honesty of mind and soul behind it.

It is a great prayer, because it confesses frankly it cannot understand why God allows what He does allow, but it will not let God go. It is prayer wrestling with a spiritual problem and making in consequence a spiritual discovery. It demands a certain self-discipline and an honest earnestness—but the truth is, we would all make far greater discoveries of God if we took our doubts and questionings to Him, instead of to one another.

But there are bigger reasons for speaking of the maturity of Habakkuk's prayer experience. He has learned, for example, how to wait for God's answer. Childhood prayers are hurried, rushed petitions before scrambling thankfully into bed. Later, perhaps, there is more of thought and time but still the prayer ends with our Amen. It is indeed a great step forward on the way of prayer when we learn to say with Habakkuk, "I will stand upon my watch, and set me upon the tower, and will look forth to see what he will speak with me. . . . though it tarry wait for it . . . the vision is yet for the appointed time . . ."

To have learned that prayer is not ended until we have finished speaking *and listening*, and to have outgrown the impatience which demands an answer immediately and in our terms—is to have learned a maturer faith more worthy of Him to Whom we pray.

To build us, as Alexander Whyte says, a tower of expectation, and believe there *is* an appointed time, is the way to far deeper prayer-experience. "I came to see" says the saintly James Fraser, great Scottish preacher and exponent of the spiritual life, "I came to see that the answers to my prayers were all but thrown away upon me". And Whyte comments that this is often so; either because we do not expect an answer (listening being no part of our praying) or because we do not recognise the answer when it comes; or because we could not wait. The fire and passion of our urgent pleading die away, and when the answer comes we are a thousand miles from the intensity and importunity of the hour of prayer: the answer oftentimes passes unnoticed.

Yet a man cannot live by immediate answers to every urgent prayer. Faith as it grows develops a long perspective—

becomes a faith with hope at the heart of it, endurance in its bones, patience in its bloodstream, resolution in its muscles. In prayer like Habakkuk's such adult, steady faith finds voice and patience to speak with God about perplexity and wait for His reply.

III

The answer Habakkuk receives is unexpected, provocative, at first sight no answer at all. "The just shall live by his faith"—in contrast to the wicked who live by pride and un-righteousness. The just shall live by his faith! As so often the Bible word is too big for a single translation, and most of the versions have put one half of the meaning in the text and the other half in the margin. He shall live by *the faith that keeps him faithful:* by the steadfastness of character that springs from trust, by the faithfulness that roots its strength in God. "Faith kept faithful keeps him finely true". Faith shall itself be his armour, his refuge and his comfort; faith, lived by, shall preserve him in face of darkness and doubt. And such fidelity of trust and character is its own best evidence, its own surest certainty, its own highest reward.

"How shall a man keep his faith?" was Habakkuk's question. His faith shall keep him, is the gist of the answer. In one sense, of course, it is an evasion of the intellectual problem of the existence of evil. Much more needs to be said—and the prophet is not without hints of some other parts of the answer. We must ponder deeply the reality and the fearful implications of human freedom. We must remember the milis of God and the hidden forces of divine justice. We must recognise frankly the partiality and the limitations of our viewpoint. And we must sit long at the foot of Christ's cross and penetrate the *glorious injustice* of that divinest tragedy, and the meaning of vicarious suffering, before we shall come within sight of the full Christian answer to Habakkuk's problem.

But Habakkuk is not in search of a philosophy: he wants

rather to understand his God. And he learns that the puzzles of faith are not always resolved with intellectual and logical finality—*though be it remembered they are nothing to the insoluble riddles that beset unbelief.* God does not explain His ways to us unless He pleases. Sometimes He *kindly* veils our eyes. Sometimes He has much to say to us but we do not pause to listen. Oftentimes the questions remain, but not the doubts. We do not understand, but we are surer of God—and that He doeth all things well. We may not have found slick explanations and facile arguments, but we have found courage, and trust, and steadfastness of character: a faith to live by.

And this again is faith in its maturity. It is not a naïve, childish trust in the immediate triumph of every good cause, in the automatic reward of virtue, in the direct issue of innocence in prosperity and happiness, of sincerity in unshadowed success. This kind of faith soon dies, or passes into something deeper—with persecution, loss, endurance and a cross in it. Yet to go on believing, amid frustration and perplexity and unanswered questions, that God is God, and right, and wise, and kind—that is a clear-eyed, realistic, adult attitude which is only learned on the watchtower of honest prayer, where a man waits upon God for resolution of his doubts. "This is the victory, even our faith."

IV

The final mark of Habakkuk's maturity emerges in the matchless closing words of the Psalm of thanksgiving. It is important to translate the glowing words into modern equivalents.

Habakkuk is saying that though harvests fail and food is scarce and dear, though unemployment and poverty stalk the land, and trade shall dwindle to bankruptcy; though mines and shipyards be idle and mills and factories stand silent—and all the might of an implacable foe "fierce as evening wolves" be loosed upon the land—yet will I rejoice in the Lord! Though all be taken, and the petition remain unanswered, still the just shall live by his faith.

This is truly the high-water mark of this type of faith. Yet there is another type, even in the Scriptures. Jacob bargained with God at Bethel—"If God will be with me, and will keep me in this way that I go, and will give me bread to eat and raiment to put on, so that I come again to my father's house in peace, then shall the Lord be my God".

The writer of the 73rd Psalm allows us to see his own transition from this immature outlook, which regards God as the universal provider, whose function it is to keep us out of trouble, to the deep awareness of God's majesty and glory. He was troubled, he says, by the prosperity of the wicked, their ease, and health, and unshaken pride; he questioned whether his own conscientiousness was worth while. Then in the sanctuary he came to understand first how slippery and shallow prosperity is; and then how priceless was his own position— "I am continually with thee: Thou hast holden my right hand. Thou shalt guide me with thy counsel, and afterward receive me to glory. Whom have I in heaven but Thee? And there is none upon earth that I desire beside Thee. My heart and my flesh faileth: but God is the strength of my heart and my portion for ever."

From this is but a step to Habakkuk's sublime "Though the fig tree shall not blossom, neither shall fruit be in the vines; the labour of the olive shall fail, and the fields shall yield no meat; the flock shall be cut off from the fold, and there shall be no herd in the stalls: yet will I rejoice in the Lord, I will joy in the God of my salvation. Jehovah, the Lord, is my strength, and he maketh my feet like hinds' feet, and will make me to walk upon mine high places."

v

Hinds' feet indeed! Steady, swift, sure-footed, climbing feet, walking in safety upon high places where others are afraid. By climbing his watchtower to expostulate with God and listen to His replies, Habakkuk has learned much that lifts the soul above the doubts and arguments of lesser minds. His is the prayer that can with humble earnestness question God's ways, pour out its perplexities in supplication for light, wait for the answer and know it when it comes, believe deeply and be strong, and so find the profound faith that can lose all and still keep God. For he has found the final truth about the life of faith, and about the experience of prayer: *the truth that faith needs no other argument than its own inherent value; that "faith is the substance of things hoped for, the evidence of things not seen"; that in fact the just shall live by his faith.*

JEREMIAH: THE NOBILITY OF PRAYER

"*Now the word of the Lord came unto me, saying, Before I formed thee . . . I knew thee . . . I have appointed thee a prophet unto the nations. Then said I, Ah, Lord God! behold, I cannot speak: for I am a child. But the Lord said unto me, Say not, I am a child: for to whomsoever I shall send thee thou shalt go, and whatsoever I shall command thee thou shalt speak. Be not afraid because of them: for I am with thee to deliver thee, saith the Lord. Then the Lord put forth his hand, and touched my mouth; and the Lord said unto me, Behold, I have put my words in thy mouth: see, I have this day set thee over the nations and over the kingdoms, to pluck up and to break down, and to destroy and to overthrow; to build, and to plant. . . . Thou therefore gird up thy loins, and arise, and speak unto them all that I command thee: be not dismayed at them, lest I dismay thee before them. For, behold, I have made thee this day a defenced city, and an iron pillar, and brasen walls, against the whole land, against the kings of Judah, against the princes thereof, against the priests thereof, and against the people of the land. And they shall fight against thee; but they shall not prevail against thee: for I am with thee, saith the Lord, to deliver thee.*"

JEREMIAH 1: 4–10, 17–19

"THE MOST CHRISTLIKE CHARACTER IN THE OLD TESTAMENT" —so Jeremiah has been described, and in many ways the tribute is justified. He stands out in spiritual stature above all the long line of godly men in Israel. He enshrines in himself the deepest and most inward truth that

Judaism ever attained. He carried a crushing burden with a heroism unexcelled even in Israel's annals. He pointed the way forward with a certainty of insight that lifts him above all other prophets. And yet he suffered intensely, bitterly, and very deeply for every conviction he held. It is perhaps in his lonely and poignant suffering that he reminds us most of Jesus. It is a tragic injustice that this man should have become a symbol of pessimism, his very name a by-word for tearful prophecies of doom and enervating lamentation.

The misrepresentation of his truly heroic spirit rests entirely upon the accidental and quite unfounded association of his name with the five poems of "Lamentations"—and can only linger where his story is unknown. He is neither miserable, morose, nor soured—nor any of the things popularly attributed to him. He looked on the joys of others gladly and even with envy, and if his certainty that they would be short-lived made him sad, that is due to his sympathy and the times in which he lived, and not to any defect of character.

Lest this defence of his greatness seem over-done, let us weigh one unquestionable historic fact. Six and a half centuries before Christ, the attention of the world was centred on the names of two would-be world dictators, Nebuchadnezzar and Pharaoh-Necho, on the clash of two great empires, Assyria and Egypt, on the bronze curtain of suspicion, fear and intrigue that divided East from West of the known world—yet nowadays, who cares? Out of all the turmoil and distress of a hundred years of war only one figure remains who influenced the history of the human spirit, and still matters to us today. And he the oddest, unlikeliest, most obscure actor on that turbulent stage, the prophet in little Judah, with taut nerves, thin skin and a lion's heart.

I

The *time* of Jeremiah was a time that called for greatness. He saw the decline and fall of Judah. Only the merest remnant remained of the great nation Solomon had consolidated, and that remnant had been subject to foreign domination for a hundred years. Geography (that set Israel between Assyria and Egypt), history (that saw the centres of power and political civilisation moving westwards to the Mediterranean) and inner decay (social, political and religious decay in Judah) all conspired to make the end inevitable. Jeremiah saw it. His fifty years of ministry were the last fifty years of Judah as even a nominally self-governing state.

It is debatable whether to live in the springtime of a nation, or in its autumn, is the severest test of characters. For Jeremiah it was late autumn, with the blasts of winter—the last winter—bearing down upon the little, proud and independent people. He could not possibly see success: the writing was too plain upon the walls. He was to be counsellor and prophet to the decayed and weakened rulers of a decaying nation in a decaying age—"A wonderful and horrible thing is come to pass in the land; the prophets prophesy falsely, and the priests bear rule by their means; and my people love to have it so: and what will ye do in the end thereof?"

He deplored their unpreparedness, denounced their stupid lack of foresight, condemned their policies toward Assyria, their false expectation of help from Egypt. Yet all the time he grieved for their fate and suffered with them and for them all the agonies of imaginative sympathy, and later actual ill-treatment. Certainly the time demanded greatness of soul, of faith, of courage, and Jeremiah had them all, as well as a longing to save his people. But the divine word was irrevocable—"Pray not thou for this people, neither lift up cry nor prayer for them, neither make intercession to me: for I will not hear thee."

II

The *task* of Jeremiah was a task that demanded greatness. It was his duty and misfortune to be always saying the "wrong" thing. In his early ministry, when danger threatened, others offered comfort and recalled the promise of the great statesman-prophet Isaiah that Jerusalem should be inviolate. But Jeremiah denounced the sin of Judah, comparing it with ruined Israel's, called Judah an unfaithful bride, and spoke of invasion and divine judgement. And no one listened to so unattractive a message from so inexperienced lips.

When good king Josiah, with the help of the law-book discovered in the Temple, set about a national religious reform, the young prophet appears to have remained silent and aloof, probably because he felt it too shallow, too royal, and consequently too shortlived, to give it his support. "They have healed the hurt of my people lightly, saying, Peace, Peace, when there is no peace". He came to suspect the religion that is based simply on the letter of the law, understood only by those who could read, and interpreted by those whose interests lay in institutional religion. "How do ye say, We are wise, and the law of the Lord is with us? But behold the false pen of the scribes hath made of it falsehood".

Later, at any rate, he came to see that only a radical reform in which the law of God should be *written on the heart* would ever succeed. Jeremiah's attitude to Josiah's reform movement remains one of the puzzles of the Old Testament, but if it puzzles us, how much more perplexing and exasperating it must have been to his contemporaries—would nothing please this fault-finding preacher?

Then when Josiah died, and the Temple became the centre of a new enthusiasm, Jeremiah is still not satisfied. "Hear the word of the Lord, all ye of Judah, that enter in at these gates to worship the Lord. Thus saith the Lord of hosts, the God of Israel, Amend your ways and your doings, and I will cause you to dwell in this place. Trust ye not in lying words, saying, The Temple of the Lord, the Temple of the Lord, the Temple of the Lord are these" (probably, "is the thing").

"For if ye thoroughly amend your ways and your doings; if

ye thoroughly execute judgment between a man and his neighbour; if ye oppress not the stranger, the fatherless and the widow, and shed not innocent blood in this place, neither walk after other gods to your own hurt, then will I cause you to dwell in this place . . . Behold ye trust in lying words that cannot profit. Will ye steal, murder, and commit adultery, and swear falsely, and burn incense unto Baal, and walk after other gods whom ye have not known, and come and stand before me in this house, which is called by my name, and say, We are delivered; that ye may do all these abominations? Is this house, which is called by my name, become a den of robbers in your eyes? Behold I, even I, have seen it saith the Lord. But go ye now unto my place which was in Shiloh, where I caused my name to dwell at the first, and see what I did to it for the wickedness of my people Israel.

"And now, because ye have done all these works saith the Lord, and I spake unto you, rising up early and speaking, but ye heard not; and I called you but ye answered not: therefore will I do unto the house, which is called by my name, wherein ye trust, and unto the place which I gave to you and to your fathers, as I have done to Shiloh. And I will cast you out of my sight, as I have cast out all your brethren, even the whole seed of Ephraim."

Such a sermon as this, delivered as it was in the Temple porch, containing every note that would most anger the men of Judah, and attacking their very religiousness in the name of the Lord, was bound to evoke the sharpest derision and hostility. It seemed that neither the absence of religion, nor religious reform nor now religious zeal and devotion to the Temple, would satisfy him. To make his position worse, a threat from Chaldea which Jeremiah had underlined had been withdrawn, and his authority as a prophet was consequently discredited, his warnings ridiculed.

As the end drew nearer his counsel was nevertheless sought by certain of the rulers, and secretly by the king, too scared to ignore Jeremiah and too weak to obey his word. Always the advice given strikes the unwelcome note. Neither the Egypt-alliance party, nor the Assyrian party will accept his reading of the situation, and his warning that Jerusalem will fall is, in the light of Isaiah's word, rank heresy. Besides, another self-styled prophet, Hananiah, contradicts the man of God, claiming superior inspiration. What a tangled, tortuous duty was laid upon his earnest heart!

As doom approached Jeremiah could only counsel sub-mission—"surrender, and be safe: resist and you will be destroyed; this is the word of God". To publish such a message was to "spread alarm and despondency", "careless talk", and treason. Prophecies of defeat, disaster and exile were a danger to morale. Jeremiah was arraigned for treachery and im-prisoned. Superstitious reverence for one who might after all prove to be a prophet prevented his being put to death, though a perilously swampy dungeon and a starvation diet were allotted to him. If he *died*, none could be blamed for *killing* him! Kings, princes and counsellors plotted against him. They destroyed the written messages he sent by Baruch out of prison, and rejected his warnings to come to terms, while still they might, with an overwhelming and implacable foe.

Assyria marched westward at last, and Palestine became the cockpit of the struggle between Egypt and the East. Jerusa-lem fell. All who were worth taking were carried off to exile, and the city was sacked. Events had completely vindicated the work of Jeremiah, and he might have found revenge in a complacent "I told you so". Instead he elected to remain, an old man now, with the aged and poor in the ruined country-side to comfort and to guide.

But even yet he is unpopular. He cannot but oppose a new and utterly foolish resistance movement among the ruined remnant, and when it fails and its sponsors flee for their lives, he is forcibly carried off to Egypt with them. There, once more, he is the centre of controversy for God. Against the prevailing idolatries of Egypt, and especially against the back-sliding of these twice-defeated but unteachable refugees into the worship of the Queen of Heaven, Jeremiah ardently pleads for loyalty to Jehovah. He is stoned to death for his pains.

It was a tragic end to a tragic career, a career that by all usual standards failed, and failed disastrously. He loved his people—"Oh that my head were waters, and mine eyes a fountain of tears, that I might weep day and night for the slain of the daughter of my people!" He lived that they might be restored to safety and to the covenant mercy of their God. But he died at the moment of their utter defeat, while the gulf between them and God yawned at its widest, with no sign of hope to comfort his breaking heart. And he knew from the beginning that it must be so. Truly his was a task that de-manded greatness.

III

And what of the man who was called to bear this prodigious burden in a tragic time? A steadfast, brave, undaunted faith, with Isaiah's lofty calm or Elijah's fearless aggressiveness? Emphatically, No! For this immeasurably painful duty in an age of turmoil and despair the call of God came to a shy, reluctant, introspective soul, fearful, uncertain, lonely, reserved, a nervous and modest country-lad, son of the keeper of a village shrine, unused to and unwilling for the shifts and pressures of political life in the capital city. Perhaps even more urgently than his time, and his task, his *temperament* demanded greatness—or else the most abject and complete failure must result.

We look in vain for any heroics, any exulting in the task, any sustaining sense of divine authority. He remains—to all appearance—throughout his life an ill-adjusted, tortured, un-happy failure of a man, his spirit too easily dejected, his skin too thin, his response to the call too unwilling ever to make a "hero". He is called in youth, and at once objects that he is

145

but a child, and afraid of men's faces. He remains unmarried, by divine decree, a sign to his contemporaries that it was no time for domestic delights; but repeatedly the sound of bridal feasts echoes in his poetry, and he felt keenly the loss of home and shelter which his often bruised and always burdened spirit might have found in human love.

To such a spirit unpopularity, the sense that every man's hand and heart were against him, was itself a cross. Suspicion of his motives, false accusation of "falling away to the Chaldeans", and misrepresentation of his words hurt him more deeply than they would a more robust soul. Of courage he had plenty, as his rewriting of the burned roll of prophecies, his sternness to Hananiah, his stout insistence on the unwelcome truth to Zedekiah, his undaunted rebuke of the crass follies of the dregs of the nation in Egypt, all make plain. But it was the courage that nevertheless shrinks with horror from physical violence; and to be placed in the stocks, kept under house-arrest, flung into prison, buffeted in public, half-drowned in mud, were experiences that lacerated without mercy a nature as sensitive and sympathetic as his. Some men would find escape in a blaze of angry defiance: Jeremiah was simply crushed.

Most poignant of all, in the secret places of his soul his own faith sometimes clouded over as the result of his suffering, and he lost his sense of the goodness of God. This was his private inward agony, unguessed by his opponents but multiplying tenfold the pain of his own conflict. More than once he regrets his birth; "Woe is me, my mother, that thou hast borne me, a man of strife and a man of contention to the whole earth! I have not lent on usury, neither have men lent to me on usury; yet every one of them doth curse me".

He protests that he did not desire to bear such a message: "Behold, they say unto me, Where is the word of the Lord? let it come now! As for me, I have not pressed thee to send evil, neither have I desired the woeful day; thou knowest, that which came out of my lips was before thy face. Be not a terror

146

unto me: thou art my refuge in the day of evil." In these words the reluctance with which he first accepted the call to be a prophet rises again in a plea to be excused, that God will not press him to go on with it.

Later he comes to such extremity as to curse the day on which life was given him: "Cursed be the day on which I was born: let not the day wherein my mother bare me be blessed. Cursed be the man who brought tidings to my father, saying, A man child is born unto thee: making him very glad. And let that man be as the cities which the Lord overthrew, and repented not: and let him hear a cry in the morning, and shouting at noontide; because he slew me not from the womb; and so my mother should have been my grave . . . Wherefore came I forth out of the womb to see labour and sorrow, that my days should be consumed with shame?"

Considered alone such feeling seems hardly worthy of a man of God, yet in one further passage his burdened heart plunges even deeper into doubt and spiritual anguish. "O Lord, thou hast deceived me, and I was deceived: thou art stronger than I and hast prevailed: I am become a laughing stock all the day, every one mocketh me. For as often as I speak, I cry out; I cry, Violence and spoil: because the word of the Lord is made a reproach unto me, and a derision, all the day. And if I say, I will not make mention of him, nor speak any more in his name, then there is in my heart as it were a burning fire shut up in my bones, and I am weary with forbearing, and I cannot contain."

Here is a man very close to all of us: one who feels acutely the rejection of his message and his work, faces a stern duty with a spirit too weak to sustain it, treads a bitter path with faltering steps, experiences all the lights and shadows of faith and doubt, with never a success to cheer his soul, and all his service of God an inward struggle that oft-times descended into mental agony. Only superb courage, integrity and tenacity of purpose could have saved such a temperament, in such a time, from absolute despair.

147

IV

Inevitably the question arises, was the man, in this particular case, matched with the hour? Did God choose aright the servant for the task? Faith says, it must be so. But the surest answer lies in the results attained. And the outcome of Jeremiah's experience is priceless gain, for out of his long Gethsemane he bequeathed to the world an inestimable threefold legacy—an imperishable story, an imperishable book, an imperishable promise.

The *story*, of course, is his own personal story of lonely, costly, consecrated loyalty to God, to truth, to right, though all men derided and all events seemed to disprove. Though all inclination, feeling and desire fought against the dictates of his sensitive conscience, Jeremiah maintained a lonely loyalty that falteringly and tearfully held straight on, feeling every failure, tasting all the bitterness, but never giving in. He trod the way of Christ centuries before Christ came, and trod it nobly.

The Bible would be immeasurably poorer without his record. It has heroes of another kind, brave, stout hearts, fearless martial spirits, bold thinkers, daring innovators, venturesome explorers in new fields, and tireless evangelists of the good news. But it has not another quite like Jeremiah. We need his splendid story when the heart dies down and mists of doubt gather in the mind, when the way is tortuous and the burden sore. We have all thanked God sometime for the ringing shouts and trumpet blasts of the mighty ones. But occasionally we thank God also in more subdued and humble tones, for Jeremiah's tears, and honest outbursts when the heart is overcharged. We know that if he held right on, we also may.

The imperishable *book*, of course, is the Book of Jeremiah, the first and in some ways still the greatest charter of personal religion. Before Jeremiah, religion was largely a social, tribal, communal, national affair. Even the reformation he witnessed was a royal deed within a state religion. But Jeremiah knew that the ultimate things in religion could not be enacted by kings, nor written in a book. He learned, as no one before him had ever done to the same degree, that while formal and public worship has its due value and function, the inner heart of all religion lies in a lonely, isolated, individual surrender to the will of God, however costly, and a lonely, isolated, individual faith in the faithfulness of God, however hidden. Because he learned *that*, in the fires of his own conflict and the loneliness of his own task, Jeremiah could place no reliance on a reformation that left the heart unchanged and the life untouched by the fires of God.

Ezekiel takes up Jeremiah's theme on the side of individual responsibility to God. Some of the Psalmists expound the joys of individual faith in God's great goodness. John the Baptist demands the preparation for the Messiah which only individual repentance and conversion can provide. Jesus declares that the kingdom of God is within you. The Christian evangelist appeals for a personal faith in Christ as the individual's Saviour and Lord. But it is Jeremiah, who in the furnace of his own affliction and the tension of his own implacable conscience prepared the way for all the later thought. He wrote the first declaration of spiritual freedom, experience of God, and personal faith that singled out the individual from the tribe, the nation and the race, and set him on his own feet before the throne of God.

And therefore, finally, his third inestimable legacy is the imperishable *promise* of the New Covenant. Standing at the end of Israel's independent existence as a nation, Jeremiah witnessed the punishment of God upon an apostate and obdurate people, and the apparently final failure of the high hopes of David's reign, of the lofty aspirations of Samuel's vision, of the profound intentions of Moses' establishment of the nation's religion on the basis of God's gracious covenant. Aware (as

Jeremiah undoubtedly was) of the full significance of what was happening about him, the prophet had every justification for crying over the city, the nation and the future "Ichabod—the glory is departed" and writing off a thousand years of divine preparation, planning and performance, since Abraham was called from Ur, as a glorious experiment that failed.

Instead, we have this: "Behold the days come, saith the Lord, that I will make a new covenant with the house of Israel, and with the house of Judah: not according to the covenant that I made with their fathers in the day that I took them by the hand to bring them out of the land of Egypt; which my covenant they brake, although I was an husband unto them, saith the Lord. But this is the covenant that I will make with the house of Israel after those days, saith the Lord; I will put my law in their inward parts, and in their heart will I write it; and I will be their God, and they shall be my people: and they shall teach no more every man his neighbour, and every man his brother, saying, Know the Lord: for they shall all know me, from the least of them unto the greatest of them, saith the Lord: for I will forgive their iniquity, and their sin will I remember no more.

"Thus saith the Lord, which giveth the sun for a light by day, and the ordinances of the moon and of the stars for a light by night, which stirreth up the sea, that the waves thereof roar; the Lord of hosts is his name: if these ordinances depart from before me, saith the Lord, then the seed of Israel also shall cease from being a nation before me for ever. Thus saith the Lord: If heaven above can be measured and the foundations of the earth searched out beneath, then will I also cast off all the seed of Israel for all that they have done, saith the Lord. Behold the days come, saith the Lord, that the city shall be built . . ."

The new covenant will thus include the implanting of the law, and the will to obey it; a new relationship of God and people; knowledge of the Lord, and the experience of complete forgiveness, and then restoration. This Jeremiah can promise, although (as we have seen) no sign is given in the life and situation of Israel of any hope for the future. He rests his expectation, not upon any foregleams of repentance and a better mind—for these are absent—but upon the steadfast will of the Creator God upon whom the changeless processes of nature and the stability of the universe depend. In other words he appeals not to any relationship of God to Israel, which might be affected by Israel's unfaithfulness, but to the original and ultimate relationship of God to creation itself. And to that unwavering, tireless patience by which in spite of all the backsliding of His people, God will yet achieve His purpose.

This is the height of Jeremiah's faith—unshaken trust in the steadfastness of God's purpose, and unshaken confidence in the permanence of truth. "All the remnant of Judah . . . shall know whose word shall stand, mine or theirs." But in both respects it was a faith sifted amid tossing doubts, and wholly unsupported by evidence in the life of the people.

This prophecy of the New Covenant is the highest point reached, along this particular line of divine revelation, the line of deeper and more intense personal religion. It forms one of the "growing points" in Judaism from which the Christian Gospel proceeded to fresh truth and fuller experience. Together with his book and his personal story it forms a heritage from the dark days of Judah's decline without which we should all be infinitely poorer.

To have achieved such heroism, insight and foresight is Jeremiah's glory, an attainment that makes even his suffering and conflict abundantly worthwhile. Small wonder then, that when "on the night on which He was betrayed, Jesus took bread . . . and after the same manner He took the cup and gave it to the disciples" it was of the lonely, forsaken, tortured, martyred prophet that Jesus was thinking as He said "This cup is the cup of a new Covenant in My blood. . . ." At that moment Jeremiah surely received his well-merited reward.

v

But what has all this stirring and subduing story to do with prayer? Nothing, and everything. Nothing, if we think only of petitions and requests, for there is little indeed of formal intercession and supplication in Jeremiah's book. When Jeremiah talks with God it is more often to pour out his burdened heart and plead for release from his responsibilities. But if we remember that prayer is the relation of a soul to God; that

> Prayer is the soul's sincere desire,
> Uttered or unexpressed,
> The motion of a hidden fire
> That trembles in the breast.
>
> Prayer is the burden of a sigh,
> The falling of a tear,
> The upward glancing of an eye
> When none but God is near,

then we realise that just as surely as Habakkuk illustrates the high-watermark of prayer as an intellectual struggle for faith, so *Jeremiah illustrates the pinnacle of prayer as a spiritual struggle for uttermost consecration and loyalty at uttermost cost.* As "to labour is to pray" so assuredly "to suffer is to pray" when the suffering is nobly borne. Jeremiah began as a child, afraid, "like a gentle lamb that is led to the slaughter"; he was made a defenced city, an iron pillar, and brasen walls—despite his feelings—because throughout fifty years of conflict, bitterness, struggle, failure and shadows, God was his refuge, strength, and exceeding great reward.

DANIEL: THE OBSTINACY OF PRAYER

"It pleased Darius to set over the kingdom an hundred and twenty satraps . . . and over them three presidents, of whom Daniel was one; . . . then this Daniel was distinguished above the presidents and the satraps, because an excellent spirit was in him; and the king thought to set him over the whole realm. Then the presidents and the satraps sought to find occasion against Daniel . . . Then said these men, We shall not find any occasion against this Daniel, except we find it against him concerning the law of his God. Then these presidents and satraps assembled together to the king, and said thus unto him, . . . All the presidents, satraps, . . . counsellors, governors . . . have consulted together to establish a royal statute . . . that whosoever shall ask a petition of any god or man for thirty days, save of thee, O king, he shall be cast into the den of lions. . . . And when Daniel knew that the writing was signed, he went into his house; (now his windows were open in his chamber toward Jerusalem) and he kneeled upon his knees three times a day, and prayed, and gave thanks before his God, as he did aforetime."

DANIEL 6: 1–10

WE ARE NOT TOLD WHAT DANIEL PRAYED, ONLY THAT he did so. It is the fact, rather than the content, of his prayer that is significant, and this is a distinction which Daniel shares with one other—Saul of Tarsus. Of him also it is written "Behold, he prayeth" without reference to the burden of the petition; and in his case also the fact that he prays at all is the focal point upon which the whole story hangs. Saul's praying signalised a total change of heart and life and allegiance which was to have tremendous consequences for the Church and for Europe. Daniel's praying epitomises a steadfast tenacity of character, an obstinate refusal to desert the faith of his fathers even in the royal court of Babylon, a dauntless spirit of religious devotion which—even when Temple, altar, festival and fellowship were no more—could still run up the flag of private prayer and hold on, and hold out.

In its way the ultimate result of Daniel's obstinacy in prayer is hardly less important than in Paul's case. For it was to just this spirit of unswerving loyalty to the Hebrew faith and vision, on the part of a small remnant of the Jewish exiles in Babylon, that the preservation of Judaism was due. Out of that exile, with its baptism of idolatrous sensuality, Jewish religion emerged purified, uncompromisingly monotheistic, morally chastened, with a new form of worship—the synagogue—a new Bible, the law and the Psalter, and the memory of an experience that gave new meaning to the ideas of God's holiness and judgement.

It might so easily have been otherwise. Law, history, poetry and prophecy, the cohesion of the nation, the hope of mercy, might so easily have perished and the people become merged with the rest of Babylon's many tributary streams of captives. But there were a few—scholars, saints, scribes, teachers, poets, a prophet or two, Nehemiah, Ezra, "Shadrach" and his friends, Esther, Daniel—who kept faith amid appalling temptation and peril. In their souls the truth and power of Hebrew religion were fiercely tested and gloriously triumphed. They guarded with their lives the heritage of Abraham, Moses, Samuel, David, and the goodly fellowship of the prophets, for the enrichment of the future generations. And Christianity, no less than Judaism, is indebted beyond calculation to their staunchness and pertinacity—to the fact, for example, that on such and such a day in Babylon, Daniel *obstinately* prayed.

I

It was of course a rather special day, a manufactured occasion. The brilliant young Jew had risen in the king's favour from interpreter of dreams to Counsellor, President of one third of the kingdom, Prime Minister-elect, and risen far too quickly to please his rivals and enemies. In spite of the temptations inseparable from his position, the character of Daniel was secure from malicious slander or corruption. The conspirators who sought his downfall paid him a glorious tribute by their exasperation—"We shall not find any occasion against this Daniel, except we find it against him concerning the law of his God". This was the only point at which he might resist the king, endangering his position and his life: and they clearly anticipated that he would do it.

And so the plot was framed. The king's vigilance and judgement were somewhat foolishly overborne by flattery and by numbers, and the pointless but unalterable decree was signed. It enacted that "if any man shall ask any petition of god or man for thirty days, save of the king, he shall be thrown into a den of lions." "And when Daniel knew that the writing was signed, he went into his house; (now his windows were open in his chamber towards Jerusalem) and he kneeled upon his knees three times a day, and prayed, and gave thanks before his God, as he did aforetime."

Of course it all turns upon that open window. This is one of the tremendous trifles of Scripture. The shepherd's "rod" of Moses, a sling and five smooth stones, "old cast clouts and rotten rags", a boy's lunch, a widow's mite, an alabaster cruse, a cock crowing, a kiss in a garden, a rolled stone are among many other little things which in Scripture story are big with meaning. Daniel's open window is a simple historical detail that defines and dignifies a character, brings a touch of relief and promise to a whole sad period of sacred history, and affords a glimpse into a hallowed room, a heroic life, a devoted heart. For the window was *already* open. Daniel simply continued to do in the day of crisis what it was his habit to do, and consistency gave him courage. He merely remained the man he always was, and found himself a hero.

II

It is easy to be lyrical about that open window high above the street in Babylon. Of course it was for Daniel *a window of vision*. It looked out across the broad Euphrates, over the rolling plains of one of the most fertile valleys in the world. Yet it was not for the view that it stood open, but because away five hundred or more miles to the south-west lay Jerusalem. Though Daniel stood next to the throne in the vast heathen Empire of Babylon, he was still a captive in spirit, an exile whose heart was in the far-off homeland, a soul whose roots were deep among the old and cherished sacred things. He remained unmoved in his loyalties by success or advancement, valuing still the eternal springs from whence his people had drunk their inspiration.

That window opened towards home, and not only in a literal way. Through it Daniel saw beyond the immediate here and now of Babylon, the long-told glories of a great history and a great faith, before which the wealth and luxury, the power and pomp of Babylon paled to tawdry cheapness in the light of God's future and God's purpose.

In this way also it was Daniel's *window of escape*. The sights and sounds of Babylon, the great idol temples and imposing processions, the immense and often lewd wall-carvings, the riot of drunken revelry and debauchery in the luxury-loving heart of a rich land, and beneath it all the murmur of complaint from those who suffered beneath the oppression and cruelty of a ruthless despotism—all this must daily weigh upon the heart of Daniel. It added sorely to the cares of office, the malice of his enemies, the constant concern for fellow-Jews less favoured. In this room he found relief, escape, freedom of spirit, and victory over Babylon.

That resolutely open window symbolises a soul's refusal to succumb, rising superior to its surroundings and its cares, finding its relief in God. To a Samuel Rutherford, "a cell with a window is a sitting-room". And every great soul that has triumphed over temptation, persecution, and dismay, has had somewhere its secret window of escape, its lattice opening towards God, where the spirit has breathed a purer air, and the heart has found the wings of a dove to bear it to the land of far distances.

Yet not alone his own escape in mind and spirit, but the return and restoration of his people, sustain the heart of this prince among exiles. Necessarily, his open window is a *window of hope*, for otherwise his tenacity is purposeless. He believes in the future, believes that it will not always be Babylon, and captivity, the constant friction with an alien environment, the grave reproach upon the name of the Lord. There will be deliverance, the re-emergence of the shattered nation, in God's good time, the resumption of the ancient covenanted purposes.

That is why it was important to keep faith. If Daniel ever had his days of doubt, the window must have closed. But Daniel "believed God", and believed that the day would come when all the might and glory of Babylon would become a fading memory, an archaeologist's reconstruction. And so the open window symbolised the open future, the flying curtains became flags of a triumphant faith in the mercy and power of God who should yet redeem His people. And Daniel *"gave thanks"*.

And so his neighbours and his enemies understood it. His window marked him out, gave his rivals their opportunity of evil. The open window is inevitably a *window of witness*, declaring to all who pass by, "Here lives a patriot". It distinguishes one who owes allegiance to other laws than Babylon's, with a birthright in another city, a spirit nourished on another heritage, an oath upon his soul to another, more glorious King. So those who desired his ruin knew how to proceed, understood perfectly where his first loyalty was anchored, for Daniel did not hide his faith from scornful eyes.

It is not necessary, oftentimes, to speak much to others of the things we believe, the principles we hold. If in the inner chambers of our lives there is a window open on the eternal world, a place of vision, a way of spiritual escape, an outlook of unquenchable hope, then the passer-by will draw his own conclusions. He will know where our love and loyalty lie, and come to understand the sources of our peace.

III

And the window was the window of Daniel's prayer-room, where of long habit he had spoken with his God three times a day. "As he did aforetime" is the impressive phrase in this heroic tale, even more impressive than the attempts of the hoodwinked king to undo his folly, or the cool courage of Daniel in the den of lions, or the "happy ending" so beloved of childhood days. For one feels that a night in a den of lions might mean comparatively little, or at any rate be nothing new, to a man of faith and integrity who had survived, and advanced to power, amid all the pressures and tensions, threats and intrigue, sin and corruption, of the Babylonian court!

It is Daniel's unbending obstinacy of faith, his sustained defiance of all that beset his integrity in that antagonistic environment and high position, which makes him one of the great men of the Exile. His window, in addition to what it means to his own heart, and because of that, becomes also the symbol of resistance to all ungodliness and compromise.

So much might have closed that frail but significant lattice— the increasing dignity and advancement of his office might have quietly drawn it to: it very often does. The winds of popular derision and polite scorn might have blown it close: we like the breeze behind us. Simple expediency, buttressed with prolific arguments about the value of having a Jewish leader in high places playing his cards astutely, knowing when to be wisely silent, tactfully diplomatic about his private principle, might have kept the hinges oiled—the window sometimes open, oftener slightly ajar, sometimes tightly shut and barred; so it is with most of us. The sudden, stupid edict of the king, imperilling all that he had worked for and attained, might well have slammed it shut.

But none of it happens. Daniel resists. He defies all that would rob him of that link with things his soul held sacred. He refuses to be stifled in the stuffy, narrow circle of the court of Babylon. He values his freedom higher than his position, his soul more precious than his life. He fastens the window immovably open and dares Babylon to do its worst. *That* is the spiritual obstinacy that preserved Judaism during the Exile, and harvested the fruits of a thousand years of spiritual pilgrimage and revelation for all future generations.

Daniel defied a heathen empire, just to say his prayers. We cannot help remembering Arthur in the school dormitory keeping to his knees as boots fly about his head. Many will be thinking of the crucial decision about a Testament beside a barrack-room bed, a hospital pillow, or in the works' canteen. So little a thing can mean so much, a mere porthole on eternity.

Prayer signifies so many things, but this not least in importance: a window on the spiritual world. It provides an outlook of vision above and beyond this realm of time and sense and sin; an outlet of escape from care and encircling temptation; an outreach of hope in dark, frustrating days; an outshining of witness to a shadowed, burdened world; an out-thrust of defiance in the name of the Lord; and withal a secret and a spring of spiritual endurance that makes men marvel.

Our fathers argued much about the perseverance of the saints. Whatever we make of the more abstruse aspects of that high doctrine, this at least is plain: one half of that conception might be renamed, the patience of God; the other half is certainly the sheer obstinacy of a praying heart. Nor is the explanation of this source of enduring strength hard to seek. It is what we might call the immovable steadfastness imparted by equal and opposite pressures.

Our ancient cathedrals, standing for centuries amid the storms of time and the shock of change, are miracles of balanced stresses. The counterweight of pillar and buttress lends solidity to turret and tower, the counter-strain of paired thrusts imparts strength to arch and groin. Even so, in a day of threat and criticism Jesus urged the disciples to balance the outward pressure of the world's hostility by the inward thrust of prayer, the downdrag of environment by the upreach of supplication. "It is impossible but that offences will come. . . . He was demanded of the Pharisees when the kingdom of God should come . . . first must He suffer. . . . Men ought always to pray, *and not to faint.*"

That was Daniel's secret. To meet the pressure of the world not merely with a brave face but with a praying heart is to achieve that staunch spiritual obstinacy which the world can neither understand nor overthrow.

NEHEMIAH: THE PRACTICE OF PRAYER

"*The words of Nehemiah, the son of Hacaliah. Now it came to pass in the month Chislev, in the twentieth year, as I was in Shushan the palace, that Hanani, one of my brethren, came, he and certain men of Judah; and I asked them concerning the Jews that had escaped, which were left of the captivity, and concerning Jerusalem. And they said unto me, The remnant that are left . . . are in great affliction and reproach: the wall of Jerusalem also is broken down, and the gates thereof are burned with fire. And it came to pass, when I heard these words, that I sat down and wept, and mourned certain days; and I fasted and prayed before the God of heaven. . . . And it came to pass in the month Nisan, in the twentieth year of Artaxerxes the king, when wine was before him, that I took up the wine, and gave it unto the king. Now I had not been beforetime sad in his presence. And the king said unto me, Why is thy countenance sad . . . Then I was very sore afraid. And I said unto the king, Let the king live for ever: why should not my countenance be sad, when the city, the place of my fathers' sepulchres, lieth waste, and the gates thereof are consumed with fire? Then the king said unto me, For what dost thou make request? So I prayed to the God of heaven. And I said unto the king, If it please the king, and if thy servant have found favour in thy sight, that thou wouldest send me unto Judah, unto the city of my fathers' sepulchres, that I may build it. And the king said unto me . . . For how long shall thy journey be? and when wilt thou return? So it pleased the king to send me; and I set him a time.*"

NEHEMIAH 1: 1–4; 2: 1–6

161

WE BEGAN OUR SERIES OF STUDIES WITH THE SUGGESTION that because prayer is the innermost heart of all religion, and therefore essentially a personal experience, it could only adequately be studied biographically, by listening to the men of prayer and watching the outcome of their praying in their life and work. The only disadvantage of this method is its concentration on the greatest men and the outstanding moments of crisis, opportunity and decision. And so our last biblical hero is fittingly a man of somewhat different type, not indeed less great or less important in his own way, but one of less notable gifts and more ordinary achievement, essentially a practical man.

Nehemiah was after all no thinker, poet, leader of thought, prophet, teacher or martyr. He built a wall, albeit an important wall. And his monument is in bricks and mortar, and a charming—if somewhat garrulous and self-occupied—book. The profounder possibilities of the prayer-life are, in his case, focussed upon the detailed concerns of an almost mundane task. Prayer's vast and varied effects are, in him, seen in qualities and deeds within the reach of the most unspectacular lives.

This does not in the least belittle Nehemiah's work, nor minimise his place in the sacred story. It is meant only to emphasise his very realistic attitude in the whole matter of prayer—his practice of referring each decision and opportunity to God for guidance at the moment of immediate need, and the exceedingly practical outcome of this attitude in the work he did for Judah and for God.

I

Nehemiah's story is familiar. His eminent position as butler to the Emperor and his retention of Jewish faith amid the pressures of a heathen environment closely resemble those of Daniel, except that now Artaxerxes was master of the empire, and the relations between the conqueror and the conquered appear to have been eased. There was business between Jerusalem and Shushan, and the Persian policy of resettling displaced peoples in their own lands was already taking shape.

There came to Nehemiah at Shushan his brother and other friends from Jerusalem, with news about the state of the fallen city and the few poor folk still living about the ruined site. Their description so affected Nehemiah that he prayed for help to approach the king, with a view to being appointed for the rebuilding of the city. It was a dangerous request easily misrepresented as an attempt at rebellion, but it was granted.

Gathering materials and documentary authority, Nehemiah set out for Jerusalem, secretly inspected the city-ruins, collected workers from among the sparse population of the scarred district, and began the rebuilding of the walls, as the first step towards making the city safe for habitation. Immediately, opposition arose from certain leaders of nearby peoples whose interest it was that strong government should not be re-established; and that the fields of Judah with its shattered villages and defenceless city should remain an easy source of fodder and building material for themselves. The attempts to hinder Nehemiah's purpose were varied and persistent, but each was foiled, and after fifty-two days of toil the work was completed.

A serious difficulty was the cost, both of maintenance and of materials, and this Nehemiah seems to have contributed largely from his own resources. He had occasion to rebuke severely certain others who were lending at high rates of interest to the poorer workers, and he took some pride in his own refusal to be a burden upon the local people.

The protected city was then handed over to the care of Hanani, Nehemiah's brother, and Hananiah the governor of the castle, "for he was a faithful man, and feared God above many". A solemn dedication with great thanksgiving, and the beginnings of organisation for the settlement of new inhabitants, completed Nehemiah's task. It was a single, straight-forward, and valuable contribution to the reconstruction of Jewry, which while it needed nothing of high inspiration or profound spiritual experience, was well conceived, competently organised, faithfully executed in spite of serious obstacles, and triumphantly completed.

Admittedly, it was a limited objective that had been attained. The Temple was still a charred and blackened ruin, and so remained for some time. And though "the city was wide and large . . . the people were few therein and the houses were not builded". But the enormous undertaking had been well and courageously begun.

II

Such in briefest outline is the story of Nehemiah's life-work. Our interest lies mainly in the attitude of mind and the qualities of character that made it possible, and of these perhaps the one which first impresses the imaginative reader is his hopefulness.

The danger of Nehemiah's being mistaken for a would-be resistance-leader, seeking to fortify a centre for rebellion, has already been mentioned. That it was not purely imaginary may be seen from the fear in Nehemiah's own heart as he contemplated his request to Artaxerxes, and still more clearly from the threat of Sanballat and Geshem to write to the Emperor in just these terms—"It is reported among the nations . . . that thou and the Jews think to rebel; for which cause thou buildest the wall: and thou wouldest be their king. . . ." Nehemiah's own position as wine-taster is grim evidence of the fear and suspicion in which the Emperor lived, and the consequences of the lightest rumour affecting Nehemiah's loyalty.

Add to this over-all problem of obtaining official permission, the jealousies and hostility of the local leaders and national groups, and the merely political obstacles to the enterprise are seen to be forbidding. The physical obstacles are even greater. The land is poor, the crops scanty, food scarce and costly, the workers and their families can ill afford time and labour for anything but their own maintenance. Nehemiah's plan must have seemed a hopelessly impractical scheme in the circumstances.

His own tour of the ruins confirmed the dismal reports of his brother. At one place there was no room for a beast to pass, so completely had the walls collapsed. The neighbouring peoples by pillaging the houses had carried off much useful material, and the ravages of over half a century's exposure to climate, beasts and undergrowth all increased the task. The workers available were unskilled, some apparently were women.

All this, together with the nature of the materials at hand, lent a sharp edge to the derision of the enemies—"What do these *feeble* Jews? Will they revive the stones out of the heaps of rubbish, seeing they are burned? . . . Even that which they build, if a fox go up he shall break down their stone wall!" All in all, it was an enterprise to daunt the stoutest heart, and we feel a new admiration for Nehemiah's simple, direct words: "I told them of the hand of my God which was good upon me; as also of the king's words that he had spoken unto me. And they said, Let us rise up and build. So they strengthened their hands for the good work. . . . The God of heaven will prosper us; therefore we his servants will arise and build."

But if hopefulness that it could be done is the *first* impression one gets of Nehemiah, certainly the most deep and memorable is the man's wonderful resourcefulness. He has the answer to everything! There is diplomacy in his request to the king that he might be allowed to rebuild *the city of his fathers' sepulchres*, not the city of David, or the chief city of Judah, nor yet the Temple (religion being so closely allied in that time to nationalism). The motive is one of family honour and filial loyalties! Doubtless Artaxerxes would know well that more was involved than the tending of graves—but the approach is skilful and subtle, nevertheless.

The foresight expressed in his request for documents, and for requisitioning authority for the first timber, is worth noting, as is the careful study of the extent of the problem *before* attempting to engage the interest of the workers. The first answer to Sanballat, that God was with them, whereas Ammonites and Arabians had no portion, nor right, nor say about the matter, is restrained and yet sufficient.

In the arrangement and allocation of the workers something not far short of sheer genius is revealed. The Tekoites repaired one spot although "their nobles put not their necks to the work"—the sharp and informed comment of an energetic foreman. Baruch "worked earnestly". The priests were set to repair the gate by which the sheep had from time immemorial entered the city for the sacrifices—who could better have been allotted that stretch of wall? Princes, rulers, goldsmiths, apothecaries, perfumers, merchants and even princesses, we are told, worked harmoniously side by side at the menial tasks, which says much for them and a great deal also for the man who inspired them.

Each had his own section of the work to do, and not all were equal. Some had gates, doors, towers, others the straight wall; and five times we are told that the work appointed was to repair the wall "next his house"—a fine incentive to speed and thoroughness. One man had apparently no ruined house in which to find temporary shelter, but he lodged in a single chamber against the broken wall—and repaired next to that room. Some worked so well that "another portion" fell to them before the work was done. Here is a cluster of lessons for all builders of God's kingdom; but also a splendid record of a prosaic job extremely well organised.

In the repulse of opposition Nehemiah shows a like ability to find the right reply. Mockery, contempt and despising are met with a fine toss of the head: "Hear, O our God, for we are despised: and turn back their reproach upon their own head" . . . "So we built the wall . . ." A conspiracy to break into the unfinished defences on all sides is met by arming each worker with sword as well as trowel, and setting a lookout, with a trumpeter standing by to give the alarm.

And so the work went on: "we made our prayer unto our God, and we set a watch against them day and night." Journeys out of the city for water were made under armed escort, and all slept within the city at night for safety. Bitter complaints against the financial stringency and the advantage being taken of it by the wealthy, find Nehemiah unexpectedly stern, and able by strong words and excellent example to resolve the crisis among his people. The cunning stratagem of his enemies, in the four-times-repeated invitation to a conference in one of the unsheltered villages is met with the splendid, unanswerable "I am doing a great work, and I cannot come down". The threatened report to the king of incipient rebellion he answers with the lie direct—"There are no such things done as thou sayest, but thou feignest them out of thine own heart"—and it appears that the courage of this reply sufficed to end the matter.

One who had been confined in some way (possibly as mad, since according to lingering superstitions about madness, the "possessed" sometimes spoke God's word) was bribed to counsel Nehemiah to seek personal refuge in the safety of the Temple ruins. "And I discerned, and lo, God had not sent him, and he pronounced this prophecy against me: and Tobiah and Sanballat had hired him". The purpose may have been to lure Nehemiah to a place of seclusion for attack, with the second possibility that such a step would spread panic among the rest, and leave him open to a charge of sacrilege. "And I said, Should such a man as I flee? and who is there that being such as I, would go into the Temple to save his life? For this cause was he hired, that I should be afraid, and do so and sin, and that they might have matter for an evil

THEY TEACH US TO PRAY

report, that they might reproach me. Remember me, O my God. . . ."

It is surely this resourcefulness that makes the character of Nehemiah so attractive and impressive—and so fundamentally practical. He seems never at a loss, never taken in, never dismayed or frightened once the task begins. "He can do all things" through God who enables him. It is a quality sadly rare, and much to be envied. For it is the simple answer to the widespread modern discouragement before great enterprises which we dignify by the name "frustration".

Two smaller elements in the quality of the man may be isolated within this general attitude. He shows a splendid determination, a resolute persistence against continually renewed difficulties. This is, of course, the stronger side of his undiscouraged hopefulness, his belief that it could be done, and would be done, if he kept right on. It is a simple virtue, but an invaluable one in life's practical affairs.

The other "smaller element" is his honourable pride in what he is doing. Rarely indeed can we mention any form of pride among religious virtues. It is a dangerous feeling, very easily degenerating into conceit, or corrupting into self-righteousness. Now and again, as we read Nehemiah's account of his work, we are a little surprised at an almost naïve air of being pleased with himself: it is never really more than that. But underneath it is a real and just sense of the dignity rightly belonging to God's work and those who do it.

"The God of heaven will prosper us: therefore we his servants will arise and build . . . I am doing a great work and I cannot come down. . . . Should such a man as I flee?" A due measure of such legitimate pride in one's responsibility and privilege in the service of God is not wholly out of place, and would sometimes save us both from indecorous and "cheap" undertakings, and from too great self-depreciation.

III

Hopefulness, resourcefulness, determination, pride—these are homely virtues, after all. Compacted together in a man neither brilliant nor inspired, they yet served to make an excellent worker in the cause of God, one of whom it is somehow typical that his life-work and monument should be the building of a wall. Others might with equal appropriateness erect for their memorial Temples, spires, lecture-halls, palaces, music-galleries or oratories. But to have built a wall out of rubbish, a wall within whose protection and shelter all lovelier things could flourish—this also is worth while.

But if the wall was really typical of the leader of the work, then there must be, here and there, a quiet alcove, a smoother place, where for a moment men might pause and pray. For this once more was the essential secret of the character of Nehemiah. He was not eloquent in prayer, as Solomon or Hezekiah; not profound and moving as Abraham or David; his praying was like all else about him direct, plain and practical. One prayer is recorded at a little length, the rest are merely mentioned, but both sorts are remarkable.

The recorded prayer is Nehemiah's reaction to the sorry news of Jerusalem's plight. It is unexpectedly full and thoughtful, and it seems peculiarly fitted to express in chosen words the penitence of exiled Judah on the eve of her deliverance. The greatness and faithfulness of God are the basis of the petition, and the earnestness of the asking is unmistakable. The confession of personal and national sin is explicit, and has direct reference to the known and admitted law given through Moses. The promise of regathering for a repentant people is believingly quoted, and the request made for God's help in obtaining favour in the sight of the king.

"I beseech thee, O Lord, the God of heaven, the great and terrible God, that keepeth covenant and mercy with them that love him and keep his commandments: let thine ear now be attentive and thine eyes open, that thou mayest hearken unto the prayer of thy servant, which I pray before thee at this time day and night, for the children of Israel thy servants, while I confess the sins of the children of Israel which we have sinned against thee: yea, I and my father's house have sinned. We have dealt very corruptly against thee, and have not kept the commandments, nor the statutes nor the judgements, which thou commandedst thy servant Moses.

"Remember, I beseech thee, the word which thou commandedst thy servant Moses, saying, If ye trespass, I will scatter you abroad among the peoples: but if ye return unto me and keep my commandments and do them, though your outcasts were in the uttermost part of the heaven, yet will I gather them from thence, and will bring them unto the place I have chosen to cause my name to dwell there. Now these are thy servants and thy people whom thou hast redeemed by thy great power and by thy strong hand. O Lord I beseech thee, let now thine ear be attentive to the prayer of thy servant, and to the prayer of thy servants who delight to fear thy name: and prosper, I pray thee, thy servant this day, and grant him mercy in the sight of this man."

This is a truly impressive formulation of the new mood of a chastened and penitent people: even so it is directed straight to its immediate purpose and the existing situation. Nehemiah is just nothing if not practical.

And this is the point, also, about the final thing to be said of Nehemiah's praying. He is the Old Testament's one exponent of what is sometimes called "ejaculatory prayer"—arrow prayer—the swift, immediate, unprepared cry of the heart to God at the moment of emergency. "Then the King said unto me, For what dost thou make request? So I prayed to the God of heaven. And I said unto the king. . . ." That swift prayer between the question and the answering is wholly in keeping with all else in Nehemiah, and is the sufficient explanation of that hopefulness, resourcefulness, persistence and dignity which we admire in him.

A man constantly in touch with God will always show just these qualities, and in the ordinary, prosaic, even hum-drum affairs of a working life he will achieve unexpected success. It is not enough to say of Nehemiah that he is a man both of action and of prayer. He *mingles* the two, hardly pausing in his acting to offer his prayer, and seemingly, sometimes, hardly pausing in his prayer to set on foot his next precaution or issue his instructions. He turns in one breath from describing the malice of the opponents to his "Hear O my Lord what . . ." "We made our prayer and set a watch . . ."—"But now, O my God, strengthen thou my hands"—"So I prayed to the God of heaven . . ."—"Remember, O God, Tobiah . . ."—such pithy, precise prayers are scattered throughout the book and enshrine the very spirit of the man.

God was to him active, real, and *at hand*, One to whom he turned instinctively at each moment that some problem arose, some new move of the enemy was revealed, some new need presented itself. And here, let it be said again, was the source of that remarkable adequacy which marks his whole career. He—and God—are ready for anything.

And on this note we fittingly close our studies of the great men of prayer of the Old Testament. For here we are without a doubt at the heart of the matter. What Micah called walking humbly with thy God: what Paul meant by "pray without ceasing"; what the whole New Testament means by fellowship with God, the communion of the Holy Ghost; what the saints of the Church have called the practice of the presence of God, this is the practical essence of the prayer-life. Prayer has its high moments of ecstasy, its depths of abasement, its breadth of implication, and its varied consequences. *But in the end Nehemiah's day-to-day experience of God as active, real, and at hand is the substance of all godliness, the centre of all religion, and the meaning of the life of prayer.*

171

Spurgeon is reputed to have said that he could not pray for long if his life depended on it; which echoes Augustine's "we may pray most when we say least, and pray least when we say most". Jesus warned us against vain repetitions, offered in the belief that we shall be heard for our much speaking. Nehemiah's arrow-prayers have much to teach us about this constant, unfailing sense that God is near and available and needs no elaborate address to receive His immediate help. If we learn it well—not forgetting the other things that others teach for other occasions—then we, too, shall find that for every daily task "our sufficiency is of God". And we shall remember, with a new understanding, the word of our Master, "Men ought *always* to pray. . . ."

The life of prayer is too rich, too deep, too intimately related to the manifold needs of men and the infinite fullness of God, ever to become stereotyped in fixed patterns of experience. The lessons which the Old Testament men of prayer have read to us are consequently varied, setting forth its richness from diverse points of view. Yet when all is said, the result falls short of the ultimate truth of prayer: for that we must turn from the great men of prayer to the Master of prayer Himself, and—like the disciples—first listen to His praying, and then with reverence and longing echo their petition, "Lord, teach *us* to pray".

PART II

THE MASTER OF PRAYER

JESUS: THE QUALITY OF PRAYER

"And when ye pray, ye shall not be as the hypocrites: for they love to stand and pray in the synagogues and in the corners of the streets, that they may be seen of men. Verily I say unto you, they have received their reward. But thou, when thou prayest, enter into thine inner chamber, and having shut thy door, pray to thy Father which is in secret, and thy Father which seeth in secret shall recompense thee. And use not vain repetitions, as the Gentiles do: for they think that they shall be heard for their much speaking. Be not therefore like unto them: for your Father knoweth what things ye have need of, before ye ask him. After this manner therefore pray ye: Our Father which art in heaven, Hallowed be thy name. Thy kingdom come. Thy will be done, as in heaven, so on earth. Give us this day our daily bread. And forgive us our debts, as we also have forgiven our debtors. And bring us not into temptation, but deliver us from the evil one. For if ye forgive men their trespasses, your heavenly Father will also forgive you. But if ye forgive not men their trespasses, neither will your Father forgive your trespasses."

MATTHEW 6: 5–15 (R.V.)

"THE PRAYING CHRIST", SAYS JAMES STEWART, "IS THE supreme argument for prayer" and inevitably our studies of great souls at prayer lead us at last to the feet of Jesus. It is no accident that in listening to the men of prayer of the Old Testament the name and thought of Jesus have never once been far away. Almost always the lesson each has taught

175

had found its echo and fulfilment in a word of Christ, and even where in the cases of Elijah, Solomon and Habakkuk the circumstances are very different from any that faced Jesus, we have still had occasion to remember Him.

In the same way we shall find echoes of each previous lesson in this one, for on this, as on all else, the Lord Jesus Christ is God's final and perfect word. His example and His sayings have been familiar from our childhood days, and yet it must be confessed that much that He showed us of the life of prayer is still beyond the range of our experience. Much that He patiently explained still puzzles us—so slow are we to learn. Our perplexities about unanswered prayer, our unreadiness to tread the new and living way which He consecrated for us into the Holy Place, our frequent echoing, when conscience reproaches us for prayerlessness, of the disciples' cry "Lord, teach *us* to pray!"—all underline our need to learn again from Jesus the simple secrets of this sacred exercise, in which all the resources and comfort of heaven are linked with the frailties and limitations of human life, and mere man holds traffic with eternity.

I

It would be impertinent to try to trace the development of our Lord's experience of prayer. He is seen in the Gospels as One whose soul's very breathing was a constant prayer. But the steps by which He came to that unbroken and unshadowed awareness of the nearness of His Father are hidden from us, as much by the shallowness of our own insight as by the mysteries of His divine person.

It is wrong, too, to speak unguardedly of "Jesus' example in prayer". In the last resort His praying was the unique praying of the incarnate Son, and into all its power and depth we simply cannot follow Him. Only He would claim, for example, "Father, I know that Thou hearest me always". He prayed neither for forgiveness, nor for light, nor for increased consecration, and in these three omissions, rightly measured, we begin to perceive the gulf that separates our prayer-experience from His. The gulf becomes plainly impassable when we hear Him say, in the Upper Room, "Father, I will that . . ." Here is prayer with an *authority* which we can never know.

With this caution against applying to ourselves things that could be true only of Jesus, we must nevertheless (if we are to understand His prayer-life at all) take very seriously the great truth of the incarnation. "The Word was made flesh", taking "the form of a servant, and being made in the likeness of men". "He hath suffered, being tempted". He was touched with the feeling of our infirmities, in all points tempted like as we are—without sin. "It became God, in bringing many sons to glory, to make the Captain of their salvation perfect through suffering . . . though He were a Son, yet learned He obedience through the things which He suffered, and being made perfect He became the Author of eternal salvation unto all them that obey Him." He is not ashamed to call them brethren, saying: "I will declare Thy name unto my brethren, in the midst of the Church will I sing praise unto Thee"; and again, "I will put my trust in Him". "As the children are partakers of flesh and blood, He also himself likewise took part of the same". And all this that "He, by the grace of God, should taste death for every man".

Into all that this means we cannot here attempt to enter. But that incarnation involved for the Son of God not only hunger and thirst, weariness and sorrow, but temptation, discipline, spiritual growth and obedience, living by faith and tasting of death, these scriptures explicitly declare. It is small wonder that the Epistle to the Hebrews can also describe Jesus as One who "in the days of His flesh, when He had offered up prayers and supplications with strong crying and tears . . . was heard in that He feared."

Our Lord's prayer-life was intensely real, whatever puzzles

theology might pose for us. We might have assumed from the absolute honesty of Jesus that no pretence could lurk about His hours of prayer, that the agonising supplication in Gethsemane could never have been mere play-acting. But the testimony of the whole New Testament makes the assumption into certainty. Our Lord was truly Man: not of course one of us—hence the great gulf between His prayers and ours; but one with us, in the nature and need of our humanity. And as Man He really shared with us the life of prayer.

II

And how He prayed! At His baptism, as He made His full response to the call that had come to Him, *He prayed*; in the busy, crowded days in Galilee, rising a great while before day to be undisturbed, *He prayed*; in the wilderness, snatching another rare opportunity for quiet, *He prayed*. As He brake the bread for the multitude, and afterwards when some would forcibly make Him king, *He prayed*; before the choosing of the twelve, again when at Caesarea Philippi He questioned them about the progress of the work, and when they returned from their mission to the villages, *He prayed*. Heading southwards for the final challenge to Jerusalem, He lingered among the hills in Galilee for prayer and was transfigured and fortified.

As Peter faced his own testing-time, Jesus prayed; and in the Upper Room He prayed for them all. Before distributing the sacramental bread He prayed again, and later in the Garden facing out the full horror of the cross, three times He prayed. And as He had lived in constant prayer, so He died—"Father, forgive them . . . Why hast Thou forsaken me? . . . Father, into Thy hands . . ." All this, be it noted, is remembered and set down, though the record is far from complete, and a habit so constant called for little repetition in the story.

It is much more true of Jesus than it was even of Jeremiah that His life was His prayer. "To think of God once in a while was a sin to Jesus". Except for the one unfathomable moment of His final atonement on the cross, the sense of God's reality, nearness and love was never absent from His soul. To Him—as indeed to us—prayer was but faith becoming articulate, love telling its love. All nature, life and history to His eyes were alive with God, and He lived in the unbroken, and unseeking, assurance that God's hand was over Him.

The darkness of the wilderness, the solitude of the mountains, the fury of the sea, the hatred of men, the betrayal of friends, the threat of Herod, the conspiracy of rulers, all found His trust unshaken, His sense of the divine ordering of His "day" unfaltering. He was in love with God, delighted to do His will, satisfied with His favour. And out of His own inmost knowledge He could declare that to find God and live under His rule is to drink wine, enjoy a feast, stumble upon treasure, discover a rare gem, sit at the marriage supper of a prince. Such was the peace, the poise, the plenitude of power, the deep joy, which prayer meant to Jesus.

Thus to the unshared uniqueness of *authority* we must add, as the marks of Jesus' prayer-partnership with the Father, a clear unquestionable *reality* of experience, and an all-sufficient and joyous *intimacy* of communion. By the help of prayer He, a true man among men, worked out His appointed destiny as the Redeemer of the world: and in His experience we see what wondrous heights the life of prayer can reach.

III

In the light of that ideal of the life of prayer, we ourselves are left stumbling somewhere very far behind, in urgent need of other—and more elementary—help. Our attempting is so fitful, our achievement so far short of our attempting. Sometimes even the answers to our prayers add to our perplexities. The answer does not come, or seems to come too late; or the

whole situation which we laid before the Lord changes unexpectedly and the outcome is far other than we hoped. We
turn, therefore, from the divine Example of the perfect Man
of prayer to ask what He, knowing so well our spiritual
infirmities and the slowness of our hearts, would say to us
concerning our hindrances, and the difficulties we meet, in
the practice of prayer.

It is useful to take up first this question of unanswered,
or strangely answered, prayer because a right consideration
of it can lead us at once close to the heart of our Lord's
teaching. We learn, for example, as we listen carefully to
Jesus, that there are many so-called prayers that are wrong,
intrinsically and from the outset, and simply *never could be
answered*, however earnestly or often we might offer them. It
is little short of startling to ponder the Master's severe stric-
tures upon unworthy prayers, and then to wonder if our praying
is of the kind that He describes.

There are the prayers that are offered for show—hypo-
critical, ostentatious prayers made "standing in the synagogues
and in the corners of the streets, that they might be seen of
men". Such prayer is *wrong in motive*. It has no real relation
to God at all, but is aimed at men—mere religious window-
dressing seeking human praise. And it gets what it seeks—
the opinion of the passer-by (not always a complimentary
one!). But it will get no more: "Truly I say unto you, They
have their reward", all that they will ever get!

Here certainly is unanswered prayer, we might almost say
unanswerable prayer. Nor may we think ourselves secure
from this temptation. Not only our public praying in the
assembly of the saints, but, strangely enough, even our private
praying can be aimed self-righteously at winning a good
opinion, others' good opinion of us or our good opinion of
ourselves. We can forget, even as we pray, that the One to
whom we speak is God. And God, who is ever just, will
give us what we really sought, not what we asked. The

complacent feeling of self-righteousness may be all the reward the prayer will ever receive.

The second unanswerable prayer is *wrong in attitude*, using "vain repetitions, as the heathen do: for they think that they will be heard for their much speaking". This is no humorous remark, as we sometimes read it, but a serious evaluation of the difference between pagan and Christian prayer. The pagan's gods and goddesses were unreliable, characterless beings, delighting in their power over mortals but inconstant, subject to moods, whims, and fits of jealousy. Or so the average worshipper thought of them. Thus the multiplying of the right formulas of divine names and attributes, compliments and promises of gifts, were necessary means of persuading the gods to do what was asked. Thus, too, "prayer" in paganism rapidly descended to the level of mere spells and incantations, still recited when the original meanings had been forgotten.

Utterly different is the simple relation of a trusting child to a loving and all-wise Father, a relation in which few words may express great understanding, and simplicity betoken deep confidence. To this point we must return. Here we notice only the Master's warning that prayer upon the pagan level— urging, begging, striving to persuade God to do what we fear He will not want to do, or what we secretly imagine He will for some unnameable reason refuse to do unless we pray "hard enough"—such "pagan" prayer can never be answered.

Prayer is not a method for coercing God, or controlling the powers of the spiritual world. It is the opening of the heart to a loving Father. That cannot be said too often, and until we learn it we are likely to find many of our prayers are fruitless. It is the essence of paganism to try to bring "the higher powers" into line with what we want; it is the essence of Christian prayer to seek to bring the heart into happy harmony with what we learn to be the perfect will of God.

It hardly needs to be added that God can never grant the prayer that is offered in *a wrong spirit*, as when the disciples suggested they should "pray down fire" from heaven upon the Samaritan village where Jesus was turned away. The feeling in their hearts was worthy enough in its jealousy of Christ's honour, but—"Ye know not what spirit ye are of". Such a prayer is condemned before it is offered. It is possible to pray in a spirit of envy, even of rebelliousness. It is possible to pray with the heart smarting under the sense that others have been blessed more than we. Sometimes we pray selfishly, asking for ourselves gifts and favours, or the solution of tangled situations, which could only be granted to us at the expense of others' loss, or hardship, or embarrassment. (We may ask to be *first* in an examination, to be the only successful applicant for a post, that our lad may be saved from an unhappy entanglement, whoever might get hurt!) But God has a great family, and He loves them all.

That is why the pattern prayer is in the plural—*Our* Father, give *us*, deliver *us*—for none may rightly ask self-centred blessing. It is a deeply humbling exercise to review our own prayers in the light of this solemn judgement—"Ye know not what spirit ye are of!"

Fourth of the kinds of prayer that cannot be answered, according to the mind of Jesus, is that which is offered on *a wrong basis*—like that of the Pharisee in the Temple, rehearsing his own virtues as the ground of his thanksgiving and requests. Indeed, we never even hear what his requests were going to be: for when a man approaches the throne of divine mercy in this conceited, self-satisfied way his petitions do not deserve to be recorded. They will certainly not be heard, as Jesus makes plain.

Finally there are the prayers that are unanswerable because they proceed from *a wrong foundation* of life and character. "Woe unto you, Scribes and Pharisees, hypocrites! for ye devour widow's houses, and for a pretence make long prayer: therefore ye shall receive the greater condemnation". It is a biting comment, still more moving when we recall that His own mother was a widow. The loss of the breadwinner posed a fearful problem to the widow. The necessity for immediate burial, and for money to pay for it, the wealth of the local Scribe, with his deed of mortgage and knowledge of the law, and her inability to read what she was asked to sign, all too often meant that in the confusion of her sorrow the new widow mortgaged her home at exorbitant rates of interest to the local moneylender. He was often one of those very men whose ostentatious public prayers proclaimed their loud profession of devotion to the law. With such praying even Jesus has no patience: its only answer must be judgement.

Thus we are reminded of the lesson Joshua taught us in his defeat before Ai, that prayer is the guardian of a good conscience and a good conscience the first requirement of successful prayer. In motive, attitude, spirit, basis or foundation some prayers are intrinsically wrong, and ought never to be offered. We certainly cannot earn God's blessing by the excellence of our virtue: but if our soul is out of fellowship with God through something unconfessed and uncorrected, we ask in vain—until we ask forgiveness.

IV

But, of course, not all unanswered prayers are essentially wrong. Some we might describe as right in themselves, but "inappropriate". We cannot say they ought never to be asked. But it may be that the only answer God can give is to grant the insight that will stop us asking.

The Master makes the point abundantly clear in one perfect example: "Thinkest thou", He says to Peter in Gethsemane, "that I cannot now pray to my Father and He shall presently give me more than twelve legions of angels? But how then shall the Scriptures be fulfilled . . .?" We are reminded here of Asa's lesson on the immense resources available to prayer. Jesus *could* ask such help, but He *would* not. The request for angelic deliverance was not wrong, but it was silenced by a higher purpose and a deeper insight.

So had it happened when the coming of certain Greeks desiring to see Jesus had struck the hour for His passion. "What shall I say?" He had exclaimed, "Father save me from this hour? But for this cause came I unto this hour! Father, glorify Thy name." Again a suggested prayer is turned aside, and never offered, because the whole purpose of His life made such a petition "inappropriate". In Gethsemane, we might say, the prayer is half-offered, half-suppressed. "Father, if it be possible, let this cup pass from me: nevertheless, not as I will, but as Thou wilt . . ." The Master's own "unanswered prayer" remained unanswered because in truth He never really offered it, naming it before God, but immediately adding that "nevertheless" which amounted to a swift withdrawal. Not everything that even He asked could be granted. "He saved others, Himself He could not save!"

Lest it be thought that this is one wholly exceptional example, nowhere paralleled, and arising only from the unique mission of our Lord, it is well to note a similar moment when, on quite another subject, a prayer is mentioned, but deliberately not offered. In the Upper Room the Master says: "I pray, not that Thou shouldest take them out of the world, but that Thou shouldest keep them from the evil." To request their removal from the world would not be consistent with their own need of experience, nor with the world's need of their testimony, nor with the divine purpose of world redemption. The petition is not asked but swallowed up in the knowledge that God's over-riding purpose is always best, seeking ends far greater than answers to our sometimes unthinking prayers would make possible. How very often in this respect we "ask amiss"!

"Our Father, which art in heaven, hallowed be Thy name. Thy kingdom come. Thy will be done, as in heaven, so on earth. Give us . . ." No words in Christendom are more familiar, nor could their purpose as the introduction to the pattern prayer be more plain. The Father's name, and kingdom and will—these are the first concern of all who pray the Christian way. These requests take precedence before all others, and only if these be possible do we seek that we have bread, or deliverance from evil.

So Jesus taught us to think of prayer, and many of our perplexities about the things we did not receive would be dissolved if we could rise to this high level of dedication first to what the Father wants. Much too often in our thinking "Thy will be done" sounds our regretful resignation to what cannot be helped. Emphatically this is *not* its meaning in the model prayer. Having called God "Father", and acknowledged His heavenly majesty, the heart that has learned of Jesus how utterly and completely God can be trusted, goes on immediately to ask, before all else, that what He plans shall come to pass, that whatever He would withhold shall be withheld. It is the ready and glad consent, all the more ready and the more glad because we know how confused and foolish are our own self-chosen ways. It is the surrender of the ultimate direction of our lives into hands surer, steadier, wiser and more loving than ours can ever be. But that must mean that while God will surely give an answer to all we ask, His answer must sometimes, and perhaps often, be a kindly "No". His "No" is always wiser than a "Yes" would be.

V

We pass to a third simple but oft-forgotten principle, still keeping close to the teaching of the Lord. There are prayers which, while right in themselves and appropriate enough to the purposes of God, yet are and must ever be *conditional*. Here God's answer cannot be assumed, unless the condition be fulfilled. Conditional prayers are of at least two kinds, according to whether their fulfilment depends upon ourselves, or upon someone else.

Of the former kind the simplest illustration is the prayer for God's forgiveness. Repeatedly, and with unmistakable clarity, Jesus has insisted that unless a man forgives his brother his own plea for pardon *will not be heard*. A sharp parable about two debtors underlines the point. The model prayer contains this one petition with a condition attached to it, and the condition is reiterated at the close—"For if ye forgive not men their trespasses, neither will your Father forgive your trespasses". And the saying about bringing thy gift to the altar, there remembering that thy brother hath aught against thee, and going thy way first to be reconciled, adds still further weight to this crucial teaching. The length, the earnestness, the detailed confession of our prayers for pardon are nothing to the point if the condition be unfulfilled. The unforgiving heart finds no forgiveness, however ardently it prays. We cannot deal with God on the ground of grace and with man in spitefulness—God will not permit us to. The condition stands: God wills it.

This is the simplest illustration of conditional prayer, but the principle has the widest application. Many of the promises of Scripture are based on clear conditions, not because we must first *deserve* the blessing (else should we all continue unblessed) but because in the nature of spiritual things some preparation of the soul is essential to make the blessing possible. And it is no true prayer to plead the promises and ignore the clear conditions.

The prayer for fruitfulness in service cannot be answered to those who fail to "abide in the vine", for has not Jesus said "Without Me, ye can do nothing"? The Spirit will lead into all truth those who "keep My words"—it cannot happen for those who do not. Examples are innumerable, but for some strange reason we are all reluctant to learn that cause and consequence hold true in the spiritual world, and that prayer can never be the substitute for fulfilling the conditions that make God's promises come true.

The second kind of conditional prayer is much more difficult to speak about with confidence. It is prayer whose answer depends upon the willingness of others. Often this is the sorest problem of unanswered prayer: when we plead for those we love, wayward, unbelieving, rebellious, but coveted for God. Here again the thought of anything pagan, coercive, magical in the power of prayer must be resolutely set aside. We are dealing with a holy God. The Christian call to intercede for others is set within the context of the Christian faith, and that faith declares at the outset that God made men free, free to disobey, to fall, to resist His grace, free ultimately to be lost. Never at any point does God infringe that spiritual freedom which is His highest gift to men, and men's greatest responsibility. Even the prayer of earnest love and longing for another's salvation must accept this prior condition. It is a hard lesson, but the truth is safest in these things.

Jesus prayed for Peter, before the great denial, in view of the denial, about the denial—but Peter still denied. Even the Lord's intercession could not evade the crucial test, or prevent the shameful fall. Somehow, we may believe, the prayer of Jesus entered with redeeming power into the total experience of the erring Apostle, and together with the warning, the look, and the remembrance, helped to melt the heart to penitence again. But Peter's freedom of spiritual development is part of the will of God within which all prayer is set, and the experience could not be miraculously side-stepped.

Possibly—though here dogmatism would be even less in place—possibly one sentence in the prayer of the Upper Room illustrates a similar limitation: "I pray not for the world". Certainly our Lord's intercession for the disciples proceeds on the assumption that they must "learn", "be kept", "be one", and it cannot all be done *for* them, without their own "abiding".

That our prayers for another soul intensify the spiritual forces playing on that soul for good, that we can "surround" with protective care and prayerful love a heart dear to us but far away, all Christian faith and experience make assuredly plain. When the heart for which we pray is itself already open to God's Spirit, and meets with ours at the throne of grace, we can feel certain that our intercession is a real factor in another's life. But when the heart for which we pray is careless, unbelieving, and resisting, a different situation arises. Then we have to remember that God is consistent with Himself. He cannot alter the laws of the spiritual world at our request. He will not, and consistently He cannot, save the unwilling heart.

Yet we must not lose faith, nor give up praying, if the obdurate soul still spurns the means of grace. It will help us to continue in prayer if we remember that God too is yearning for that one for whom we pray, with a love yet more eager and more deep than ours. It will help us if we bear in mind, too, that the answer to our pleading is rarely given us to see, and may be most effective when we think the situation hopeless. It *must* be right to persevere in good intent.

The point that emerges from this review of what the Master said about unanswered prayers is that there is a spiritual quality in prayer which is far more important than length, or frequency, or fervour; a spiritual quality that is essentially a matter of insight, of consecration, of surrender to God's will in the perfect, happy confidence that He wills best.

Of course this does not mean that God does not deal in gentleness with the faltering, blundering requests of His so easily misunderstanding children. We all know that He does. Our first childish prayers are often precious memories of how wonderfully the Father condescends to deal with childish hearts. But we must grow up. And if we are to think honestly about unanswered prayer, and learn the lessons God would teach us by His refusals, we must not be content merely with petulant questioning and complaint. Nor with searching for a better "technique" of prayer; nor yet with demanding more exaggerated assurances. We must remember, always, to Whom we pray. We must learn more perfectly what is His will about this wondrous privilege He has granted to His children. Above all, we must get it clearly into our minds and hearts that truly Christian prayer is prayer born of the spirit of Christ in our own lives. That means it is prayer that is Christ-like in its motive, its attitude, and its spirit; rising from a true foundation in our penitence and sincerity of conduct; in harmony with God's purposes, and mindful of His conditions.

It is futile, and unworthy, to complain that this makes of prayer an exacting and forbidding exercise. That simply is not true. But it is true that the soul's converse with God is the highest experience the human soul attains, and if in the process mind and heart and spirit are refined and stretched, can we be surprised? Jesus had certainly other things to say about the life of prayer, but this He clearly said in several ways and with solemn intent. *The most important thing about all prayer is not its words, its form, its length, its fervour, but its quality; and the most important thing about its quality is that it should rise from a spirit wholly Christ-like.* To such prayer, the Father's ear is ever open.

JESUS: THE REWARD OF PRAYER

"*Thy Father which seeth in secret shall reward thee openly . . . Ask, and it shall be given you; seek, and ye shall find; knock, and it shall be opened unto you. For every one that asketh receiveth; and he that seeketh findeth; and to him that knocketh it shall be opened. If a son shall ask bread of any of you that is a father, will he give him a stone? or if he ask a fish, will he for a fish give him a serpent? or if he shall ask an egg, will he offer him a scorpion? If ye then, being evil, know how to give good gifts unto your children; how much more shall your heavenly Father give the Holy Spirit to them that ask him? . . . What things soever ye desire, when ye pray, believe that ye receive them, and ye shall have them . . . Whatsoever ye shall ask in my name, that will I do . . . If ye shall ask anything in my name, I will do it . . . If ye abide in me, and my words abide in you, ye shall ask what ye will, and it shall be done unto you . . . I have chosen you . . . that whatsoever ye shall ask of the Father in my name, he may give it you . . . Verily, verily, I say unto you, Whatsoever ye shall ask the Father in my name, he will give it you . . . ask and ye shall receive, that your joy may be full.*"

MATTHEW 6: 6; LUKE 11: 9–13; MARK 11: 24; JOHN 14: 13, 14;
15: 7, 16; 16: 23, 24

IT WAS CONVENIENT TO BEGIN OUR STUDY OF JESUS' teaching with His comments upon unanswered prayers, because we are thus led straight to His great emphasis upon the spiritual quality of prayer, the motive, spirit, and consecration that lie behind petition. But it would be completely wrong to leave any impression that this was the main burden of our Lord's instruction. Far more is said about the prayer that will be answered than about that which will not, and some of these sayings are among the most precious we have from His gracious lips.

A few of these utterances, nevertheless, cause us some perplexity. They are so broad and explicit in assuring God's answer to the praying heart. Certainly, we want to believe them; we wish we could do so without misgivings or mental reserve. But they seem to tell of a level of prayer-experience that lies far beyond our reach. "Ye shall ask what ye will, and it shall be done unto you": that surely describes the very zenith not only of prayer-experience but of all spiritual privilege. But can we reach it?

Before we turn to these, the final, most authoritative words of all upon our theme, it will help if by way of preparation we ponder once more the prayer-experience of Jesus Himself. We have already reviewed the most significant recorded moments in our Lord's prayer life, and it scarcely needs to be added that such constancy and intimacy of communion with God lies behind all that we love, admire and worship in our peerless Master. Yet it is attractive to recall these great moments again, to seek in them the Lord's own experience of the rewards to be gained through prayer. What, in His eyes, are the "values" of prayer?

I

Keeping as closely as possible to the sacred record of His prayers, we notice first the answer which (according to Luke) Jesus received to His prayer of dedication in His hour of baptism. There came a divine Voice, attesting His sonship and mission; there descended the divine Spirit, equipping Him for His task. In some way we cannot penetrate or define, His soul attained in that hour an added assurance and certainty as to His own person and work, and the way that God would have Him tread.

A similar experience came in answer to His prayer upon the mount in Galilee, as He faced the long journey to Jerusalem and the cross. He was transfigured, God spoke, and Moses and Elias talked with Him concerning His death. In another crucial hour, when certain Greeks asked to see Him at the feast, His uplifted soul received again the answer of a heavenly Voice affirming the divine purpose concerning Himself.

Can we not conclude that these are but three outstanding instances of something happening constantly for Jesus? He found in prayer the repeated reassurance of His relationship to the Father, of His mission and authority, of His duty and the Father's care for Him. Doubt had no opportunity of entrance into His praying heart. He was never uncertain of Himself, or confused about His way. He was never at a loss with men or out of touch with God. He was sometimes more light-hearted, at other times more heavy with sorrow, but He suffered no moods such as afflict our wavering faith. Prayer was to Jesus the secret of a steadfast mind, the perpetual spring of an unfailing reassurance.

To describe such an experience is to know one does not possess it. Yet how desperately our tangled, shadowed, inconstant lives need just *this* gift of prayer!

Reverently, and with all due reserve, we may infer that part of this reassurance which came to Christ through prayer, was a certain clarity of mind about His work, and the people with whom He had to deal. It was His habit to retire for prayer after the busy, demanding day and the strife of many tongues. When in Galilee the excited crowd, fed miraculously on the hillside, would forthwith make Him king, He sent away the people and sought for Himself the solitude and silence of the hills for prayer. There, things returned (may we say it, even for Him) to a true perspective, and the dangerous moment passed.

On the eve of that crucial day when Jesus chose the Twelve, He spent the night hours in lonely prayer, coming forth to face the whole company of friends with judgement clear, and full comprehension of His men—including Judas. At Caesarea Philippi, too, He prefaced the all-important questioning of the disciples, upon which His future programme hung, with earnest prayer.

Prayer does bring, even to the busiest and most harassed minds, a clearer insight, a calmer judgement, a re-orientation of the mind to its true alignments. And if Jesus found this a rewarding gift of God, how much more precious would it be for our perplexed and burdened thoughts. In His case it was but the return to the mind's normal centre of rest, in God: in ours, it has more the aspect of daily divine guidance, and the gift of understanding what the will of the Lord is. But however we define and analyse—how much we need it!

Of a piece with spiritual reassurance and mental re-orientation is the Master's emotional restfulness. We take far too much for granted the miracle of His own peace, the unbroken calm of His spirit, the poise of His finely-tempered strength. There is always about Jesus a serenity that *imparts* the peace it offers. There is in Him a quietness of strength, with all His powers in perfect balance, that instils the calm of God and holy places. It is not that He is never moved, or angry, or distressed for others; rather is it that He always *consents* to be so, remaining in superb command. He is never restless, never impatient, never hurried, never afraid.

Yet the peace of Christ is neither fatalistic, like the Mohammedan's, nor merely negative like the Buddhist's, nor proudly indifferent like the Stoic's. It is the peace that can either ride the storm or end it, when He comes upon the lake from a mountain-top of prayer. He can be silent before Herod, commanding before Pilate, dignified before the shouting crowd, gracious even on the cross, because He has wrestled in

THEY TEACH US TO PRAY

Gethsemane alone. His peace has a positive, powerful, tenacious quality, that endures, and achieves, great things.

"Be not anxious" is His counsel. "Come ye apart and rest . . ." is His kindly invitation. "Thy will be done" is His steadying prayer. "Father, into Thy hands . . ." is His final surrender when the tempest has passed. Truly, in His communion with God He found a secret that has eluded all men everywhere—save those who have sat at His feet—the secret of the restful soul that finds its strength in deep serenity and its power in stillness of the spirit. We do not need the advice of the psychiatrist, nor the warnings of the surgeon, to bring home to us our need of inward restfulness. Our hearts cry out for it.

At risk of appearing to overdraw the picture, we must in loyalty to the sacred record make reference to two other "rewards" of the Master's praying: renewal, and radiance. Again we are at a loss to define exactly the toll upon Christ's own spirit of His daily ministry to the sick, the afflicted, the lost and the hostile. We do remember that "being weary with His journey He sat thus by the well". We recall a storm on the lake through which He slept, in the hinder part of the ship, upon a pillow. It is written that "virtue went out of Him". After a long and crowded Sabbath evening in Capernaum, He is up a great while before dawn, seeking a solitary place to pray before another day begins. He comes from the mount of prayer to the epileptic boy in the valley, with the power the disciples lacked, adequate where they were helpless. And afterwards He tells them "This kind goeth not forth but by prayer."

Again we remember that significant word: ". . . always to pray, and not to faint". Jesus found spiritual recuperation in His prayer time; His drained powers were replenished, His nervous energies were recharged, His strength was nourished and refreshed at eternal fountains. Prayer meant power, renewed power for work, for endurance, and for suffering.

And so to the remaining fact the records press upon attention: in prayer Jesus found radiance of spirit. We had foresight of this in the story of Moses, whose "face shone". We noticed then the parallel between Moses' experience and the transfiguration of Jesus. But once again the outstanding moment is but the special instance of something typical and repeated in the life of our Lord.

It was not only on the "sacred Mount" that Jesus was transfigured. He bore within His spirit an inner radiance that all too often we have missed, because we know Him as the Man of Sorrows. Yet children loved to gather round Him. His teaching has flashes of humour and poetry. He ate and drank with men, and joined in the simple festivities of rejoicing friends. Often and again He called upon men to "Be of good cheer", offering solid reasons for that injunction in the mercy and goodness of God. It could be written of Him that He "delighted" to do God's will, and we are told, too, of several outbursts of thankfulness to the Father in heaven. Once Jesus exults in spirit, over the success of the disciples' mission, and very significantly, and surely out of personal knowledge, He counsels the disciples to pray, promising the answer, "that your joy may be full."

To omit this trait from the portrait of Jesus is to distort the image of the Son of Man. He knew much of the joy of communion with God. He tasted the deep gladness of a truly prayerful spirit. Neither the greatness of His task, the hostility of men, the sins and sorrows of His people, nor the fate that awaited Him could lay His heart low: still He rejoiced in God, and spoke of the "blessedness" of life under God's rule. Only prayer *can* sustain that radiance of soul which nothing can eclipse. We learn it from Him, and wish we knew it in ourselves!

There has been nothing in all this about prayer for "things", nor about prayer for deliverance from threatening situations, or from fears. But neither has there been a prayer for mercy, for spiritual progress, or for increased consecration. Such requests are appropriate for us, and we shall see that He clearly encourages us to make them. But they are inappropriate for Him, and we recall again the gulf that necessarily separates His prayers from ours. Nevertheless, the study of what prayer meant to Jesus depicts for us the ideal level of prayer-experience, towards which we strive, and up to which God in His grace will willingly help us.

Gathering the threads together, they weave an impressive pattern of spiritual health and soundness. It is, of course, important to keep in mind the context of Christ's praying. He is no recluse, withdrawn from public affairs and exacting responsibilities to devote Himself to soul-culture. His life is set amid conflict and the clash of minds; He initiates an amazing society, originates a new world of thought, makes such an impact upon His time as affects all subsequent times. Crisis and challenge, danger and decision mark all His path. And it is in this setting that He yet can find in the exercise of prayer perpetual reassurance of soul, re-orientation of mind, restfulness of heart, renewal of energies, and radiance of spirit. Truly, prayer holds the secret of "wholeness" of life, and perfection of personality.

II

But this is the ideal. It lies, we have said, far ahead of the point which most of us have reached. Between that point, with its perplexities, disappointments and failures, and the ideal of ever-prevailing prayer, stretches a wide distance over which we need more detailed, practical and simple guidance *how* to pray. We turn, therefore, from the failures of unanswered prayer, and the ideal of perfect prayer, to seek the Master's counsel concerning prayer that is likelier to be heard. We find He has offered abundant guidance on the faith, the manner, and the content of such prayer.

For the *faith* in which to pray, Jesus reasons from the best of human fathers to the source of all fatherhood in God. Fathers worth the name do not mock their children's hunger with stones, serpents and scorpions. "If ye then, being evil, know how to give good gifts unto your children, how much more shall your heavenly Father give good things to them that ask Him?" This is more than judging God by the best in yourself: it is judging by His handiwork, as with the lilies, the grass and the fowls of the air. Surprisingly, Jesus underlines this argument by comparing God with a lazy, conscienceless Judge, and a churlish, unfriendly neighbour. Yet a widow in need gets redress by "pestering" such a Judge, and the improvident neighbour obtains his bread by "keeping on" at his unwilling friend. *How much more* will God the loving Father, the very opposite of both, give readily and generously to His pleading children? For us—as for Abraham—the argument from what God is like to what we may confidently ask provides valid foundation for our prayers.

This faith in the divine Fatherhood makes prayer simply the conversation of the spiritual family, and lends to Christian prayer its distinctive and unique tone. Paul sees in the use of "Abba, Father" a signal example of the difference Christ has made. This faith is the basis of the pattern prayer, and frames the Saviour's own address to God, both in praise and in intercession.

But the variations of the Name are all significant. Sometimes it is simply "I thank Thee, O Father". For us, in the model prayer, it is Our Father, for none can call on God exclusively. It is also "Father, which art in heaven", for though "Father" brings Him near beside us, yet is He still God, dwelling in majesty and throned in light. Reverence must mingle with our confidence. Once Jesus prays to His "righteous Father", for nothing asked of God can set aside His justice and His truth. Once again it is "Holy Father"—another solemn reminder that prayer has its moral conditions.

Always in the thought of Jesus the name Father means far

more than modern indulgent parenthood. God is still the God of all the ages, Sovereign of the worlds He made; always, in every relation to His children, the *Kingly* Father, before whom we bow in awe as well as love.

Of the *manner* in which Jesus bids us pray it is enough to recall that the purpose of the pattern prayer (according to Matthew's setting of it) was to provide a Christian model in contrast to the vain reciting of pagan religion. Its main feature therefore is to be seen in its natural, simple brevity. It contains not a single unnecessary word; it does not beg, or cringe, or even plead, and its only eloquence is the eloquence of direct approach. It is a two-minute prayer, at most, reminding us of Nehemiah's arrow prayers. Its concrete relevance to actual needs of daily life recalls the lesson Hezekiah taught us. The model prayer impresses us in other ways too, but it is this brevity and naturalness which enshrine the Master's main intention.

Not that we should never pray for longer than two minutes! Jesus spent whole nights in prayer, and the prayer of John 17 would occupy much longer. But the length should be governed by the wide horizons and the large petitions (as with Solomon's prayer at the dedication of the Temple) and not by the multiplication of words. Once more the quality of prayer is so much more important than the quantity.

As to the *content* of our prayers we have clear encouragement from Jesus to pray for certain things. Foremost among them is the repeated counsel to wield the weapon of prayer in the warfare against evil. Jesus often underlines the lesson that we learned of Jabez, that prayer offers deliverance from the power of sin; and on its other side, the lesson of Daniel, of prayer as defence against the pressure of an evil world. "Lead us not into temptation, but deliver us from evil" is suggested as the "daily" prayer of the Christian, as urgent and practical as the prayer for daily bread.

Jesus, we have seen, prays for Peter in his temptation, and for the disciples to be "kept from the evil" in the world to which He sends them. Similarly in Gethsemane Jesus urged the disciples to pray for themselves, in respect first to the certainty of temptation, and secondly to the weakness of the flesh, so easily betrayed into slumber when the crisis is upon us. In this realm certainly Jesus regarded prayer as the one great necessity, a resource and a refuge for the soul hard pressed by sin. There are times when that encouragement to pray about the sin that so easily besets us, is very precious to the weary heart.

Jesus gives clear encouragement, too, to prayer about the work of God—"touching the Kingdom". He urges that we pray the Lord of the harvest to send forth labourers into His harvest-fields. He counsels us to pray when the task becomes obviously beyond our powers, as in the case of the lunatic boy whose condition baffled disciples not yet proficient in prayer. He advises that we pray for the easing of circumstances in the day of persecution, "Pray ye that your flight be not in winter. . ."; and for the gift of endurance and survival to stand before the Son of Man. He assures us that, when the pressure of unscrupulous power becomes too great, the prayer that God would intervene to vindicate His elect shall surely be heard.

In such promises from the lips of Jesus we hear again the lessons of Moses, praying for resources for his task, of Gideon finding boldness at the throne of grace, of Elijah, finding in God's presence renewed assurance that God is still God. All prayer about the cause of God is prayer that must prevail, for it is prayer that is near to the heart of God Himself.

We have heard Jesus pray for Peter, for the twelve, and for "all who shall believe". We remember that mothers brought their children that He might pray over them; and we recall His command that we pray for those who despitefully use us and persecute us—and if for our adversaries, how much more for our colleagues and brethren. Here is warrant enough for saying that—spite of the special difficulties about this type of prayer—Jesus encouraged us to pray for others.

Against evil, about the kingdom, on behalf of others—such petitions Jesus assures us win a hearing in heaven; and asked in the faith of trustful children, in the manner of simple and natural confidence, will "find God's ear".

III

The life of prayer is altogether too sacred, and too deep to be learned in superficial haste, or without much careful thought and self-examination. We have been content with its ABC—well knowing that bigger things lie still beyond our view. We begin to leave the elementary levels, and pass to themes and possibilities more profound, when we gather together, finally, those sayings of Jesus which offer, not merely encouragements to pray in specific ways, but explicit guarantees stated in quite general terms, that prayer shall be granted.

In such sayings, some few hearts find a glorious assurance: others, but a wistful perplexity. "Ask whatsoever ye will, and it shall be done unto you. . . . If ye shall ask anything of the Father He will give it you in my name". At first sight such promises do not seem to be borne out in Christian experience, and they appear to describe an intensity of communion and an infallibility of petition which are unattainable in this life. What are we to make of them?

Among these very definite assurances are one or two that do not surprise us quite so much, and it may be that from them we may learn the right understanding of the others. Jesus promises immediate hearing, and answer, to the publican's cry "God, be merciful to me, a sinner!" Here is a prayer that always, at all times (assuming it be sincere, of course), is guaranteed success. Nor is there any doubt of the reason why; for as David found, and all the Gospel loudly proclaims, the heart of the penitent is very near indeed to the heart of God. There lies a significant clue to all these sweeping promises.

Three further sayings group themselves easily together around a common thought. "The Father . . . shall reward thee . . ." is the promise given to those who pray in *secret*, shut up (like Jehoshaphat) to "God alone". The "reward" may not be exactly what is asked, but some reward is certain when we wait alone in humble and expectant concentration in the secret place with God.

Yet Jesus clearly does not discourage *corporate* prayer, for "it shall be done for them" is the assurance given to any two "who shall agree on earth as touching anything that they shall ask". Moreover, He vigorously defended the Temple as a "house of prayer for all nations", consecrating place and time for fellowship in prayer.

To these we may add the two examples of *importunate* prayer—the parables of the unjust Judge and the reluctant friend, whose meaning is also expressed in the progressive emphasis of "*Ask* and it shall be given you, *seek* and ye shall find, *knock* and it shall be opened unto you". Here again Jesus is very definite about the answer that will come.

A moment's reflection makes clear the common factor in these three lines of thought, for each suggests a situation in which prayer becomes, as it were, sifted, refined and disciplined. Alone with God the heart is humbled, softened and enlightened, and the prayer grows purer. Praying with others corrects the merely personal, narrow, and selfish request, in the fellowship of shared zeal and sympathy. And nothing— literally nothing—purifies our prayers of the merely impulsive and unthinking demand like long delay, the need to pray again, and yet again, until our real desire is tested and only the essential plea remains. To such hearts, disciplined by solitude, or fellowship, or time, to a closer walk with God, much can indeed be promised.

The great assurance is given, once more, to those who, like Habakkuk, pray in great faith. "All things whatsoever ye shall ask in prayer, believing, ye shall receive". Mark records the saying still more boldly: "All things whatsoever ye pray and ask for, believe that ye have received them, and ye shall have them." The paradox ("Believe that you have got it and you will get it!") will not trouble those who are familiar with the Master Teacher's arresting methods of emphasis, but the apparently limitless promise given to the believing prayer does occasion some bewilderment. It seems almost to give warrant to the wildest fanaticism, to justify the boldest presumption.

The trouble lies in our habit of treating faith as an abstraction, or idea; as an optimistic state of mind, a resolute attitude of the will "looking on the bright side". We talk sometimes as though it is our great faith, and not our infinitely greater God, which does great things for us. The difference is quite crucial. Abstract faith accomplishes nothing—except perhaps a pleasant frame of mind by sheer auto-suggestion; but faith in God is a personal relationship between the heart and God, to which all that God wills, and all the surrendered heart desires, becomes gloriously possible.

Such a believing heart, believing not merely in prayer, or in itself, or in the need to be confident, but in the God and Father of our Lord Jesus Christ—with all that such faith implies of His wisdom, sovereignty and love—is a heart to which, again, much can be promised. For it is a heart in close touch with the heart of God. And such a spirit will often know, by an inner assurance given as it prays, that what was asked was "right", and will be granted: this surely is what Jesus means.

And so we come at last to those profound and gracious sayings about prayer which John preserved for us. "Whatsoever ye shall ask in my name, that will I do, that the Father may be glorified in the Son . . . If ye shall ask anything in my name that will I do . . . If ye abide in me, and my words abide in you, ask whatsoever ye will and it shall be done unto you . . . Ye did not choose me, but I chose you, and appointed you, that ye should go and bear fruit, and that your fruit should abide: that whatsoever ye shall ask of the Father in my name, he may give it you . . . In that day ye shall ask me nothing. Verily, verily, I say unto you, If ye shall ask anything of the Father, he will give it you in my name. Hitherto have ye asked nothing in my name: ask, and ye shall receive that your joy may be fulfilled. . . . In that day ye shall ask in my name: and I say not unto you, that I will pray the Father for you; for the Father himself loveth you, because ye have loved me, and have believed that I came forth from the Father."

With such words we pass, it is clear, beyond the elementary stage of learning how to pray, into the deeper realm of spiritual experience where life and prayer are truly one. The boundless promise is given, repeatedly, on certain suppositions: and the clue with which we began provides the truth with which we end. The *penitent* heart is sure of answer because its penitence brings it near to God. The *disciplined*, refined petition of the tutored soul is surer of reward. The heart whose *faith* has introduced it to the character and will of Him to whom it prays, can pray with greater confidence. So it is to those who *abide in Him*, who retain firm hold upon His words, who bear rich fruit as branches of Himself, who seek as He does only the glory of the Father, and across whose life and prayer can be written the name that is above every name. It is to those that He can say with utmost confidence, "Ye shall ask what ye will, and it shall be done for you". As at the beginning of the teaching of Jesus we are concerned with the quality of our prayers, so here at the end we find we have passed on to think of the quality of those who pray.

Beyond that we cannot go. At the earliest attempts to pray, we stand—as it were—over against God, beseeching Him to "Come over and help us". We assume the distance between us, we call upon Him to come down and deliver us. When the lessons have been fully learned and the whole way of prayer patiently trodden, we find we are standing at God's side, "abiding in the Vine", and our prayer rises no longer across a gulf, but from within our fellowship with Him. We ask no longer for the things we—of ourselves—desire: but for those that we *in Him* have learned to want.

Out of the childhood of impulsive prayer we have passed through the pain of oft unanswered prayer, into the joy of prevailing prayer, and have not noticed that it is not merely our prayers but we ourselves have changed. For God has drawn us nearer to Himself, and schooled our hearts to love what He loves, and will what He wills, because we have learned to trust Him, utterly and in all things.

"God hath sent forth the Spirit of His Son into our hearts, whereby we cry, Abba, Father; The Spirit also helpeth our infirmity: for we know not how to pray as we ought; but the Spirit himself maketh intercession for us with groanings which cannot be uttered; and He that searcheth the heart knoweth what is the mind of the Spirit, because he maketh intercession for the saints according to the will of God."

So let us pray!

CPSIA information can be obtained
at www.ICGtesting.com
Printed in the USA
BVHW041250150720
583802BV00013B/154